Responsibility

International Library of Philosophy and Scientific Method

Editor: Ted Honderich

A catalogue of books already published in the
International Library of Philosophy and Scientific Method
will be found at the end of this volume

Responsibility

Jonathan Glover

NEW YORK
HUMANITIES PRESS

Published in the United States of America 1970
by Humanities Press Inc.
303 Park Avenue South
New York, N.Y. 10010
Reprinted 1972

ISBN 0-391-0097-7

Printed in Great Britain

To Vivette

CONTENTS

PREFACE

This book puts forward a series of arguments relevant both to the traditional philosophical problem of free will and to current debates about the criminal responsibility of the mentally ill. I have sometimes put forward my own views by contrasting them with those of certain other philosophers or with those of various psychiatrists and other contributors to the psychological and legal debates. It should in fairness be said that those whose arguments are criticized may in some cases no longer hold these views. I have selected books and articles for criticism where they have seemed to be clear or uncompromising expositions of points of view, and have sometimes on these grounds preferred to discuss an older piece of work rather than a more recent one.

The reader should also be warned, with reference to the discussion of Aristotle in the first chapter, that I cannot read Greek, and that I have treated the Ross translation of the Nicomachean Ethics as though it were an English work. I have read little of the huge quantity of discussion by modern scholars of what Aristotle meant. The English version of Aristotle contains so much that is relevant to the topic of responsibility that I have felt justified in discussing it despite these disqualifications. I am grateful to Professor R. M. Hare for pointing out some mistakes here. He is not responsible for those that remain.

A key role is played in the book by the concepts of a causal law, of simplicity and of an attitude. I have relied heavily on these concepts without undertaking the very substantial work of contributing to their elucidation.

Parts of the first three chapters appeared in my B.Phil. thesis at Oxford in 1965. I benefited a lot from the stimulating and demanding standards of criticism of my supervisor, Professor A. J. Ayer. As a graduate student I also learned much from Mr Derek Osborn, who first persuaded me of the truth of some of the opinions here advanced as my own.

I have learned a lot, as will be obvious, from the writings of Professor H. L. A. Hart and of Professor Stuart Hampshire.

Parts of chapters one and three were used in a paper read to the Philosophical Society in Oxford in 1966. I am grateful for helpful criticisms made in the reply to my paper by Mr Alan Montefiore, and at the same meeting by Professor H. L. A. Hart. Much of the material of the book was used in lectures in Oxford in 1968 and 1969. Many helpful comments were made by graduates and undergraduates in the discussions that took place then. I especially remember the valuable criticisms of Mr Derek Parfit. I have so often been stimulated by discussing the subject matter of the book with others who teach philosophy in Oxford and with undergraduates I have taught, as well as with other friends outside philosophy, that I cannot name everyone who has influenced the ideas in this book. The editor of the series has forced me to make the book less diffuse and less obscure.

My wife Vivette has read and discussed each chapter. She has influenced my thinking on these questions so much that it is hard to separate her ideas from mine.

J. G.

I

THEORIES OF RESPONSIBILITY

This book is concerned with attitudes to people and to what they do. In particular it concerns questions about when it is right to praise or blame people for their actions, or to feel proud of, or guilty about, our own actions. These attitudes towards ourselves and towards other people seem to be intimately bound up with beliefs about what we call 'moral responsibility'. We are reluctant to blame or punish someone for an act of his for which we think he was not responsible, and moral praise seems equally inappropriate. Pride or guilt seem similarly misplaced where we are not responsible for our own actions.

The concept of 'responsibility' is an elusive one. The condition that blame or moral praise are only appropriate where men are responsible for their actions is obscure. How are we to decide when a man is responsible for an action? What does the word 'responsible' mean? People suffering from certain mental disorders are held to be responsible for none of their actions, or else for very few of them. Some legal systems assume that the answer to the question, 'Was he responsible for this action?' may not be a simple 'yes' or 'no', for they recognize a state of 'diminished responsibility'. But how can one tell when responsibility is diminished? Are there irresistible impulses? If so, how do they differ from impulses that merely are not resisted? Are the boundaries of responsibility so hard to determine that we should exclude consideration of it in our treatment of criminals?

Leaving aside questions of mental illness, there are many problems about the responsibility of perfectly normal people for what they do. When does ignorance excuse an action? Can it ever be right to hold a group of people collectively responsible for the actions of some of its members?

Further problems are sometimes said to be raised by advances in psychology, and in the natural and social sciences. These advances are often held to be reducing the range of actions for which people can legitimately be held responsible. It is a common view that these sciences either presuppose or give support to a determinist doctrine. It is said that moral responsibility is bound up with man not being a 'mere machine', so that it would be undermined if psychologists, neurophysiologists and others could provide mechanistic models giving adequate causal explanations of all human behaviour.

Debates on these questions of responsibility take place in isolated compartments. Philosophers bring forward *a priori* arguments for and against various theses of determinism. They discuss whether determinist claims, if true, would conflict with what 'we' normally think about human freedom and responsibility. Lawyers and psychiatrists debate with each other and amongst themselves on the relations between mental illness and responsibility, without considering the more general links between causal explanations and excuses. Reading some of the literature on responsibility, it is hard to avoid being struck by two criticisms. One is that the philosophical discussions are impoverished by their isolation, both from the sciences that study the causes of what men do, and from the medical and legal problems of devising practical tests of psychological inabilities and of criminal responsibility. The other is that lawyers and psychiatrists hold views and take decisions, both of which are distorted by philosophical assumptions. These are either assumptions about the truth or falsity, relevance or irrelevance, of some thesis of determinism, or else assumptions about what does or does not justify blame or punishment. These philosophical assumptions are often unconscious, usually unexamined, and almost always confused.

In this book, questions concerning determinism will be taken as fundamental. This is because, if determinism were both true and necessarily undermining of responsibility, all the other questions would be redundant. It will be argued that we have no adequate grounds for saying that determinism is false. Even if determinism is not true, it is never safe to assume that any particular act cannot be explained in purely causal terms. It will be claimed that many decisions about responsibility are moral ones, and thus cannot be answered merely by invoking some factual claim, such as the truth of determinism. But it will also be argued that determinism cannot so readily be reconciled with common beliefs about responsibility as some thinkers have supposed. In particular, there are problems of devising tests for psychological inability that would not, in a determinist world, be satisfied by everyone. These problems will be discussed partly in the context of mental illness and punishment. Philosophical argument is needed, both to justify our accepting some factors as excuses while rejecting others, and to give a sharper account of what it is to have impaired abilities. The results of the arguments to be put forward on these matters will be presupposed in a discussion of some attempted evasions of moral responsibility.

In this chapter, it will be argued that some questions about responsibility are moral ones, about which people with different attitudes may legitimately disagree. These questions will be approached by way of examining two philosophical accounts of when men can be blamed or morally praised for what they do. These two accounts, one put forward by Aristotle and the other by F. H. Bradley, are in some ways in agreement and in other ways strikingly different. Study of their theories sheds light both on the boundaries of responsibility and on the, perhaps more fundamental, question of what it means to say to someone that he is responsible for what he does. It is often assumed that a man's responsibility is an identifiable factor that may at any particular time be present or absent, or even 'diminished'. To be responsible for one's actions is thought of as equivalent to being in a certain mental state. English law sometimes speaks in terms of the presence of a 'guilty mind' (*mens rea*), and the Homicide Act of 1957 speaks of 'mental responsibility'. The points at which Aristotle and Bradley disagree help to bring out how far from the truth is any view that merely identifies responsibility with some mental state from whose absence one may suffer.

3

1 ARISTOTLE'S ACCOUNT OF VOLUNTARY ACTIONS

People sometimes utter words of approval or of condemnation, or mete out rewards or punishments without taking the agent's responsibility into account. It might be argued that, in cases where the agent is not responsible for the action in question, such steps taken or words spoken afterwards are not genuine cases of reward, punishment, praise or blame. But even if this contention is denied, it may be said that such steps are inappropriate. To punish a man for an action of his for which he is not responsible can be seen as inappropriate in the same way that kicking a motor car that will not start is inappropriate. Aristotle[1] held that voluntary actions were the only ones for which a person could be praised or blamed: this is the justification for treating his account of voluntary actions as an account of responsibility. He characterizes a voluntary act as 'that of which the moving principle is in the agent himself, he being aware of the particular circumstances of the action'. This is contrasted with involuntary acts, characterized as those 'which take place under compulsion or owing to ignorance'.

Aristotle discusses the compulsion that makes acts involuntary. He says that an act is done under compulsion when the cause is external to the agent, so that he contributes nothing to it, as when a sea captain is carried off course by a wind, or by men who have him in their power. It is recognized that there are difficult borderline cases, as when a man throws his cargo overboard in a storm, or obeys a tyrant to save the lives of his family. After some hesitation, Aristotle says that both these actions are voluntary, as there is a deliberate choice between alternatives, and the movement of the limbs originates in the agent himself.

Discussing ignorance, Aristotle says that an act done through ignorance is only involuntary when it causes the agent subsequent pain and regret. Other acts done through ignorance, while not voluntary, are not involuntary either. The ignorance that makes an act involuntary is of the particular circumstances or persons

[1] *Nicomachean Ethics,* Book 3, is the source of this version of Aristotle's doctrine. A more extended discussion would have to take account also of the treatment of this topic in the *Eudemian Ethics.*

4

involved, not a general ignorance of what one ought to do. (Aristotle holds that ignorance of what one ought to do gives grounds for censure and leads to wickedness.) Mitigating ignorance can be of the nature of one's action (as when a remark 'escapes' one); of a person (as when one mistakes a son for an enemy); of an instrument (as when one mistakes a pointed spear for one with a button on it); of an effect (as when one kills a man with medicine meant to save him); and of manner (as when, meaning to hit a man playfully, one really hurts him).

An important feature of Aristotle's account of voluntary actions is that it includes acts occasioned by anger or desire: on this view we are not absolved from responsibility for an act because it is impulsive. Two arguments are given for this. Aristotle holds that both children and animals always act out of desire or impulsively and yet sometimes act voluntarily; if he is correct, there must be acts that are occasioned by desire or impulse that are also voluntary. His second argument is that there are some things, such as health or learning, that we ought to desire; similarly sometimes we ought to be angry. It would be odd to make moral judgments of this kind if these desires and passions were involuntary. And, as the wicked actions triggered off by desire or anger are just as much our actions as the good actions occasioned in this way, they too must be voluntary. Actions resulting from deliberation are thus only a subclass of voluntary actions.

It might be thought that cases of drunkenness would raise difficulties for Aristotle, as he approved of punishments being doubled where a crime was committed by a drunken man, and yet drunkenness might seem to entail ignorance of the nature of one's action. The apparent inconsistency is avoided by saying that this kind of ignorance is culpable because the man had it in his power to avoid getting drunk. Aristotle considers the objection to this that a man may not be the kind of man to take care of this. His reply is that such men 'are themselves by their slack lives responsible for becoming men of that kind, and men make themselves responsible for being unjust or self-indulgent, in the one case by cheating and in the other by spending their time in drinking bouts and the like; for it is activities exercised on particular objects that make the corresponding character'. Later he says, 'to the unjust and to the self-indulgent man it was open at the beginning not to become men of this kind, and so they are unjust and self-indulgent voluntarily; but now they have become so it is not possible for them not to be so'.

The weakness of Aristotle's account of compulsion is its vagueness. When a ship is blown off course by the wind, it is clear that the captain contributes nothing to this process. But when the captain is made to change course by men who have him in their power, he might seem to be in a similar position to the man who obeys a tyrant to save the lives of his family. Yet Aristotle says that the sea captain is acting involuntarily while the man who obeys the tyrant is not. This is puzzling, since in each case there is a deliberate choice between alternatives and in each case the movement of the limbs originates in the agent himself. This criticism may be unfair to Aristotle,[1] as his example of the men who have the sea captain in their power can be interpreted in a different way. Aristotle's own words are 'if he were to be carried somewhere by a wind, or by men who had him in their power'. It might be that the situation envisaged was the one described above, where the captain still steers the ship, but under orders of a man who prodded him in the back with a sword. On the other hand, it may be held that a more plausible interpretation of Aristotle's words is to take them as suggesting that the captain is tied up while the men steer his ship. On this interpretation, Aristotle is correct in seeing a sharp distinction between the sea captain and the man who obeys the tyrant. But the sharpness of the distinction is gained at the cost of propounding a doctrine that may seem harsh, for it holds people responsible for actions done under duress. The severity of this doctrine is mitigated by Aristotle saying later that some voluntary acts that would normally bring disgrace can be condoned in special circumstances. He gives as an example the case of a man who is afraid of unbearable torture. But the circumstances that remove blame vary with the degree of the offence, and for an offence such as matricide the blame cannot be removed by any plea of extenuating circumstances.

If the making of moral judgments can be separated from the activity of giving a philosophical analysis of responsibility, it is at times difficult to know which description to apply to some of Aristotle's remarks. His doctrine of strict responsibility for

1 As Professor R. M. Hare has suggested to me.

matricide might be held to be part of an elucidation of the concept of responsibility. Although his discussion is in terms of voluntary actions, it would not be absurd to restate what he says as follows: 'We are not prepared to apply the word "responsible" to a person's action when he is afraid of unbearable torture, except in cases where his action has a degree of wickedness comparable to matricide.' This seems to be conceptual analysis, simply explaining a feature of the way in which 'responsible' is used. Someone might disagree with Aristotle's attitude towards responsibility for matricide by saying that some torture is so severe that it will excuse anything. The conflict seems to be one between severity of judgment and lenience, and as such it is not clear that it can be settled by any appeal to the meaning of a word such as 'responsible' or 'voluntary'.

Aristotle's account of when ignorance can absolve a person from responsibility is open to dispute of a similar kind. The majority of people using the moral vocabulary of our own society might agree that those kinds of ignorance listed by Aristotle as absolving men from responsibility were correctly classified in this way. But there might often be dissent from his view that general ignorance of what one ought to do does not absolve from blame.[1] It is true that this Aristotelian doctrine has echoes in our society in such maxims as 'ignorance of the law is no excuse'. But if someone holds that it should be an excuse, this is a moral disagreement rather than a conceptual one. In considering arguments on this question, one might weigh up whether or not one thought that there was a duty to know the law, as well as the possible consequences of allowing ignorance of the law to count as an excuse. One would surely be unimpressed by any attempt to rule out one view or the other by any allegation that the word 'excuse' was being misused.

It has been noted that, on Aristotle's account, impulsive actions occasioned by anger or desire can be blameworthy. Both Aristotle's attempts to justify this opinion are open to question.

1 There is an interesting discussion of this in Haksar: 'Aristotle and the Punishment of Psychopaths', *Philosophy,* 1964. The question of how we should regard actions performed in accordance with morally objectionable but sincerely held moral principles is discussed by Professor G. E. M. Anscombe: 'The Two Kinds of Error in Action', *Journal of Philosophy,* 1963, and by Professor J. Feinberg, 'On Being "Morally Speaking a Murderer"', *Journal of Philosophy,* 1964.

His first argument is that both children and animals always act out of desire or impulsively and yet sometimes act voluntarily. It is not clear what is meant by saying that animals or children always act out of desire or impulsively. If it just means that they do what they want to do, in that elastic sense of 'want' in which it can be said that any action is what the agent 'wanted' to do, then this applies to adults also. But if 'desire' is being used here in such a way that we are to understand that children and animals can never refuse to gratify such desires as for food or sex, the doctrine is surely false. Both children and animals can be taught to reject food in certain circumstances, even if they are hungry. And there is a similar difficulty about the notion of 'impulsive' action. If it is merely being asserted that children and animals sometimes act without having any rational plan in mind, then this is equally true of adults. If, on the other hand, Aristotle means that children and animals never act on a rational plan, this is again simply false. Krechevsky's[1] experiments show that rats trying to solve a problem will sometimes think of a hypothesis and act on it to see if it is true, which is almost an ideal case of acting on a rational plan. And the view that children never act on a rational plan to which they subordinate their immediate impulses could only be put forward by someone who had forgotten what it was like to be a child. Even the view that children and animals can legitimately be held responsible for what they do is open to question. It is true that children are punished when they do wrong, but many would regard this as a process of training by methods similar to those of Pavlov rather than as retribution for wickedness done by responsible agents. The same claim would normally be made about the 'punishment' of animals.

To underline the fact that Aristotle's view of children and animals is not universally accepted as self-evidently true it is appropriate to quote Bradley's account:[2]

   1   We must distinguish punishment and discipline, or
   correction; the former is inflicted because of wrong-doing,
   as desert, the latter is applied as a means of improvement.

1 'The Genesis of "Hypotheses" in Rats', *California University Publications in Psychology*, 1932.
2 *Ethical Studies*, Ch. 1.

It is right to inflict the former only in the case of a being either wholly or partially accountable. The application of the latter (which is not punishment) is a practical question for parents or tutors, both in respect of the occasion and amount. Pedagogic punishment (proper) differs from judicial in admitting greater latitude of particular considerations in the individual case.

2 If many persons meant what they said, animals are moral and responsible, and animals are punished. And a time would seem coming when we shall hear of the 'rights of the beast'. Why *not*, in Heaven's name? Why is the beast not a subject of right, civil at least, if not political? But this is for our emancipators of the future. We are content to hold the vulgar creed that a beast is no moral agent, actual or possible; it is not responsible, nor the subject of rights, however much the object of duties.

Even if one rejects Bradley's retributive view of punishment, or finds his irony unsympathetic, one can see that a plausible case can be made out for his refusal to accept that 'punishment' of a child or animal presupposes its responsibility. Aristotle's first argument in support of his belief that impulsive actions occasioned by anger or desire can be blameworthy is not persuasive.

Aristotle's second argument for this belief is that there are some things that we ought to desire, such as health or learning, and sometimes we ought to be angry. And these moral judgments, in Aristotle's view, presuppose that such desires and passions are voluntary. The claim that we ought to desire health or learning is one that is not self-evident. If a man who was ill found that he was happier than when he was well, we would be more likely to consider him strange or sad than wicked. And it is by no means obvious that a man ought to desire learning: an understanding of writers like Rousseau or Blake should undermine our willingness to accept Aristotle's apparent assumption that the value of learning is beyond dispute. As Professor Strawson[1] has said, 'Men make for themselves pictures of ideal forms of life. Such pictures are various and may be in sharp opposition to each other; and one and the same individual may

1 'Social Morality and the Individual Ideal', *Philosophy*, 1961.

be captivated by different and sharply conflicting pictures at different times.' The Aristotelian ideal of a man temperate, rational and learned is only one among the paradigms that can capture our imagination. And at times, as when meeting certain scholars or when reading George Eliot's description of Casaubon in *Middlemarch*, we are inclined to feel quite strongly that a lot of learning can be a dangerous thing.

But even if we provisionally accepted Aristotle's contention that a man ought to desire health and learning, this would by no means commit us to accepting that acts occasioned by desire are voluntary. There is a danger here of confusing two kinds of desire. To say that a man desires health or learning is to say no more than that he would like to be healthy or learned. But when we speak of sexual desire or desire for food, we are talking in different terms, for we are talking of appetites that it is inconceivable[1] that we could give up. A man who desires to be learned will perhaps be unable to give up his ambition, but it is perfectly possible, on the other hand, that a man might change his mind completely about the desirability of learning. But, without major physical changes, a man cannot abandon his hunger or his sexual desire. If we accept the principle that one only says that someone ought to do something when there are alternatives open, this may lead us to accept Aristotle's contention that acts occasioned by the desire for health or for learning are voluntary. There is no reason why we should be misled by the ambiguity of words like 'desire' and 'appetite' into supposing that acts occasioned by physical desire must similarly be voluntary.

There is a similar ambiguity in the word 'anger'. There is no need here to discuss the complicated problems of providing philosophical accounts of the various emotions, or to decide on the merits of a theory such as that put forward by James and Lange. But it should be common ground among philosophers and psychologists who have considered these problems that a word like 'anger' can be applied to several different states of affairs. One can at least distinguish between calm and violent anger, between the anger expressed in words that are contemptuous but calm and the anger expressed by flushing cheeks, trembling, and by words which, if they come at all, are incoherent and spluttered. Whether or not particular cases of calm

1 In practice, if not in logic.

anger are in any way avoidable, it is surely clear that there are cases of violent anger which are no more avoidable than a reflex jerk of the leg. In such cases, we cannot choose whether or not to be angry, and it is thus unreasonable to claim that we ought sometimes to be angry in this way. If we can choose whether or not to be calmly angry, it may be reasonable to say that sometimes we ought to have this kind of anger, but such a contention by no means establishes that acts occasioned by any other form of anger are voluntary.

Aristotle's belief that we can justly be blamed for impulsive acts done in a fit of passion is not self-evidently true. A dispute between Aristotle and someone who says that there are irresistible impulses that issue in actions for which one cannot be blamed is only partly a philosophical dispute about whether there can be irresistible impulses: partly it is again a dispute between severity and lenience. Appeals to common practice are useless in settling such an issue, just because people differ widely in their willingness to accept different excuses. 'He cannot be blamed for that: it was done in a fit of passion in which he lost control of himself' has a familiar ring, but so has the reply, 'He should not have lost his self-control.'

The final questionable feature of Aristotle's account of voluntary action is his view that we are responsible for our character. In this respect, Aristotle's view of man is surprisingly similar to that put forward by Sartre. The difference is that, on Aristotle's view, we make our character by our actions, but this process comes to an end at a point where our character is fixed, while, according to Sartre, we go on making and re-making our character all our lives, and it never becomes fixed beyond possibility of change. The Aristotelian doctrine is debatable, partly because of the vagueness of our concept of 'character'. It is not clear whether the relationship between a man's character and his actions is a causal or a logical one. At times we make remarks such as 'his generous nature makes him do a lot for other people', as though we were explaining generous actions in terms of a causal link between them and some separately identifiable generous nature. Yet at other times we assume that character can only be identified through actions, so that the link is logical rather than causal. We are confused about this because some aspects of a person's 'nature' can sometimes be identified apart from his behaviour:

if, for example, we know the state of a man's autonomic nervous system or of his glands, we may be able to tell whether he is excitable or phlegmatic or the strength of his sexual desires, independently of any observation of his behaviour.

If, when talking of a person's 'nature' or 'character', we are careful to distinguish between when we are simply referring obliquely to his actions and when we are referring to some other factors that influence actions, we will be in a better position to evaluate Aristotle's claim that we are responsible for our characters. The examples Aristotle gives of character traits are when a man is unjust or self-indulgent. If the unjust man is only a man who often acts unjustly, then the doctrine that he is responsible for this aspect of his character comes to no more than a restatement of the doctrine that, except in certain special circumstances, men are responsible for their actions. If, on the other hand, a man's frequent unjust actions are seen as being caused by some separately identifiable factor called his 'unjust character', Aristotle is taking for granted answers to questions about causation and responsibility that he never explicitly poses. If an unjust nature plays a causal role in a man's behaviour similar to that played by his blood sugar level, the existence of such a nature itself either is or is not the result of other causal factors. Aristotle seems to hold that a man's character is the result of a causal process, the important causal factors being that man's previous activities. As we have seen, he holds that 'it is activities exercised on particular objects that make the corresponding character'. But previous activities were themselves the results of choices whose outcome either was or was not governed by causal laws. If causal laws did govern the outcome of these choices, some philosophers would deny that men could be held responsible for them on the grounds that, in some sense, they could not have acted otherwise. If causal laws did not govern the outcome of these choices, other philosophers would say that they were the result of pure chance, and hence that men could not be held responsible for them. At this point it is sufficient to note that Aristotle did not discuss the problems raised by these arguments, but that, had he done so, he would have found that at least some of the possible answers were incompatible with his view that we are responsible for our characters.

Because people show different degrees of severity or lenience in considering whether to accept various excuses, it is impossible to give an analysis of responsibility that will provide a decision procedure corresponding to some universal practice in accepting or rejecting excuses. Aristotle's discussion does not claim to do this. He is concerned more with giving an account of the considerations that are relevant than with telling us exactly how to weight each consideration. But even this modest attempt cannot succeed in such a way as to give universal satisfaction, just because there is disagreement even over what types of consideration are relevant. As we have seen when considering some of the details of Aristotle's account, disputes over what considerations are relevant are often clashes between different moral standpoints.

2 BRADLEY'S ACCOUNT OF RESPONSIBILITY

F. H. Bradley[1] holds that there is a logical link between the ordinary man's concept of responsibility and the liability to punishment. He says that 'for practical purposes we need make no distinction between responsibility, or accountability, and liability to punishment. Where you have the one, there (in the mind of the vulgar) you have the other; and where you have not the one, you can not have the other.'

At the beginning of *Ethical Studies*, Bradley is concerned to analyse the word 'responsible' (or, in his own nineteenth-century phrase, to examine 'the vulgar notion of responsibility') and to see if theories proposed by determinists and libertarians are consistent with the assumptions underlying the normal use of 'responsible'. He argues that three conditions must be satisfied if I am justly held responsible for an action:

1 'I must be throughout one identical person.'
2 The deed 'must have belonged to me – it must have been *mine*'.
3 'Responsibility implies a *moral* agent. No one is accountable, who is not capable of knowing (not, who does not know) the moral quality of his acts.'

Baldly stated in this way, these conditions may seem obscure, but Bradley gives a detailed account of how they are to be interpreted.

1 *Op. cit.*, Ch. 1.

The first, that 'I must be throughout one identical person', is to be understood in a quite straightforward way as ruling out the possibility of Jones justly being held responsible for an act of Smith's. It is made clear that this condition does not allow statements like 'he is not the man he was' or 'he is a changed person' to absolve someone from responsibility. In most cases the view that I cannot justly be held responsible for someone else's actions would not be disputed. But there are some cases often counted as exceptions. Sometimes a man is held responsible for what is done by his children or by those carrying out his instructions. 'My' actions could perhaps be held to include those that result from my instructions, but it is less clear that they include those of my children. The kind of upbringing a man gives his children and the degree of control he exercises over them are important influences on their behaviour, and to the extent that their acts result from these influences they too can be counted as 'his' acts. And, just as a man can be held responsible for the consequences of his negligent inaction, so those acts of his children that result from his negligently failing to influence or control them can also be seen as 'his'. Sometimes children do things in spite of, rather than because of, their upbringing and the parental control to which they are subject, but in such cases, even if the parents are held legally responsible, they would not normally be regarded as morally responsible for these acts of their children. So these two apparent exceptions to Bradley's principle need not be regarded as serious objections to it.

The other type of case where the principle that one cannot justly be held responsible for another man's acts sometimes is challenged is where people want to hold a whole group collectively responsible for the acts of its members. The group in question may be a class of schoolchildren, or a whole social class, nation or race. Whether or not doctrines of collective responsibility are morally objectionable, there are people who hold them. Thus any account of 'the vulgar notion of responsibility' that, like Bradley's, insists that a man is only responsible for his own acts fails to reflect the diversity of common moral attitudes.

Of Bradley's three conditions for responsibility, the second, that the deed must belong to me, is the most obscure. This is because it is a vague formula standing in for what are really three quite separate conditions. On Bradley's account, a deed belongs to me when it can be said to 'issue from my will', which is contrasted with a deed done under compulsion. But even when there is no compulsion, a deed does not belong to me unless I have a certain minimal intelligence and also know, or have a duty to know, the particular circumstances of the case.

Bradley distinguishes between absolute compulsion, which is 'the production, in the body or mind of an animate being, of a result not related as a consequence to its will', and relative compulsion, which is merely the threat of absolute compulsion, and which does not absolve from responsibility. (In this discussion, 'compulsion' will denote 'absolute compulsion'.) Acts done under compulsion include those done in a state of terror or great bodily weakness, where there was no conscious exercise of the will.

An apparent inadequacy of this account of compulsion is that it seems to leave out of account the possibility of an act which results from the agent's choice but where we would often say that the choice itself was made under compulsion. One thinks here of Aristotle's example of a man who obeys a tyrant to save the lives of his family. Bradley recognizes this problem, and himself poses the question 'Can the will be forced to this or that result?' His answer is not clear:

> It all depends on the way in which we use 'will'. If by
> 'will' we mean 'choice', 'volition', the conscious realizing
> of myself in the object of one desire (in the widest sense),
> which has been separated from and put before the mind,
> as a possibility not yet real – then the will can not be forced.
> For, supposing you could produce a state of mind, which
> certainly would issue in such and such a volition, yet the
> result, when produced, comes from the self. There is no
> saying 'I did not will it'; or 'If I could have willed, I would
> have willed otherwise'.
> But if will be used (as it often must be) in a lower sense,
> then I am afraid we can not deny that the will may be, and
> often is, forced, and forced not relatively but absolutely.
> How is this? To put it shortly, it is because, by the
> application of compulsion, the psychical conditions of
> volition can be suppressed, so that it becomes impossible for
> me to decide myself for this and not for that.

It is difficult to know how this account is to be interpreted.

At the beginning of the passage, Bradley seems to hold that 'volition' is equivalent in meaning to 'choice', for he lists the two words together as part of an analysis of one sense of 'will'. Whether or not there are events properly denoted by the word 'volition' is a matter of philosophical dispute. One can avoid commitment on this issue by speaking of 'choice', for I take it that no one disputes that men sometimes choose to do things. If one summarizes Bradley's account in the uncontroversial terminology of 'choice', it remains puzzling. Bradley seems to hold that, in the ordinary sense of 'choice', no one else can compel me to choose as I do, because my choice comes from my 'self'. And yet compulsion can sometimes make it 'impossible for me to decide myself for this and not for that'. One of the examples given of this impossibility of decision is a case where someone is in a state of extreme terror. It is plausible to say of someone that he is so terrified that he cannot choose what to do, but one wonders in what way choice is impossible. Clearly choice is not logically impossible in such a case: it is not self-contradictory to say that a man is in such a state and yet manages to choose what he will do. The impossibility must be of an empirical kind; to decide between courses of action may be impossible for a terrified man in the way that to run a four minute mile is impossible for an average man. So one may concede to Bradley that sometimes choice may be impossible. It is less plausible to concede that the other part of his doctrine is true, for it seems that, when we do choose, we can sometimes be compelled to make one choice rather than another.

This point can be clarified by mentioning again Aristotle's example of a man who obeys a tyrant to save the lives of his family. Let us assume that he is not so terrified that he is unable to make a choice: he chooses to do something that he finds distasteful in order to protect his family. This might sometimes have been the situation confronting men living in Germany at the time of Hitler, who found themselves ordered to play a part in mass murder. A man might choose to co-operate with the Nazis in such circumstances, and say later that, although he chose to do this, his choice was made under compulsion. Bradley would not hold the man responsible for what he did unless it was his own fault that he was in that situation. But he would reject the view that the man was compelled to choose one course of action rather than the other. Here we can see that the word 'compulsion' is ambiguous. In one sense, it is quite legitimate for such a man to say, 'I was compelled to choose as I did', for this can be taken simply to refer to the threats against his family. This is the sense of 'compel' that Bradley overlooks. And yet, in another sense, we could correctly say that the man was not compelled to choose as he did: it was open to him to choose to sacrifice his family rather than work for the Nazis. This is the aspect of the situation that Bradley reminds us not to ignore. The distinction between these two senses of 'compel' is not the same as Bradley's distinction between relative and absolute compulsion, for his 'relative compulsion' is the threat of making a person do something without his own choice, while the threat here is of harm to other people.

Bradley's third condition, that only moral agents can be responsible, is a direct denial of Aristotle's view that general ignorance of what one ought to do is no excuse. We have seen that the disagreement on this matter between Aristotle and Bradley is a moral one. No doubt Bradley's view fits the current use of 'responsible' better than Aristotle's does, because we are often disinclined to punish a psychopath. But, if an Aristotelian were to reply that we ought to punish a psychopath, his moral recommendation could not in any way be 'refuted' by an appeal to current practice.

Having listed the criteria he considers must be satisfied for someone justly to be held responsible for an action, in the sense in which the man in the street uses the word 'responsible', Bradley mentions some aspects of the matter about which people are vague. He says that the ordinary man has no clear views about the meaning of 'act', or about for which consequences of an act a man can be held responsible. There is similar vagueness about the minimal level of intelligence that a man must have before he is responsible for his actions. There is no clear popular doctrine about whether one can ascribe responsibility in various borderline cases, such as when a man is drunk.

The present discussion of Bradley's account of responsibility has stressed his description of compulsion. This emphasis has been deliberate: it is in his account of compulsion that Bradley diverges most from views current in our own time. On most current interpretations of responsibility in our own society, we would at least not hold a man fully responsible for an action done under duress. If a man is threatened with torture unless he does some wicked action, we might readily absolve him from responsibility for it, or consider that his degree of responsibility was reduced. But, on Bradley's account, it is hard to see how such considerations could possibly be invoked in any case where the man chose to avoid the torture. It is true that he says that 'in a given case, there may be only one or two courses for me (my not acting may be a course of action); and all of these I may dislike or disapprove. But one course I *must* accept. In short, I may be compelled to an alternative; and here whether what I do is morally imputable, depends on whether it is my fault that I am in the position I am in.' This quotation is the justification for saying above that Bradley would not hold responsible a man who obeyed Hitler to save his family, provided that he was not in such a situation through his own fault. A man who had actively helped Hitler come to power would presumably be held responsible for whichever way he resolved his dilemma. Bradley's account of such a case is the account that would probably be given by most of the people in our present society who consider these matters, but it seems to be inconsistent with his general account of criteria for responsibility. The man who chooses to obey Hitler may be a moral agent, quite intelligent, and aware of the circumstances of the case. On Bradley's general account, this entails either that he is responsible for his action or else that he is acting under compulsion. But he is not acting under compulsion, in Bradley's sense, for he makes a deliberate choice. It is hard to see how Bradley can justify not holding him fully responsible.

The strict view that Bradley adopts in enunciating general principles is at odds with the lenient view that we normally adopt and which, as we have seen, even he himself is tempted by at times. The dispute between supporters of the two views resembles so many of the disagreements about responsibility already mentioned in that it cannot be settled by any evidence or by the results of logical analysis: this dispute also is one between conflicting moral attitudes.

3 THE CONCEPT OF RESPONSIBILITY

The word 'responsible' leaves more room for debate about its application than does a word like 'rectangular'. Disagreements about whether someone is responsible for his act need not be between a correct view and a mistaken one. This is partly because decisions to hold someone responsible can be criticized or defended in the light of different attitudes of varying severity or lenience. But it is also partly because there are several different uses of 'responsible'. In legal context, to say that someone is responsible for an action may be to say that he is liable to the normal legal consequences of it. To say that someone is morally responsible for what he does may be to say that he can legitimately be praised or blamed if either of these responses is appropriate to the action in question. On the other hand, a person's being responsible for his act may consist in the ability to control what he did: his responsibility in this sense may be a reason for holding him liable to legal consequences or to moral blame. [1]

There are various factors that are commonly taken to excuse one from responsibility for what one does. Aristotle's two headings of 'ignorance' and 'compulsion' cover many excuses. Beyond these, we often allow pleas of self-defence or of great provocation to be relevant, either as justifications, or else in mitigation. Other pleas are more open to dispute, and also less clearly defined. We are often reluctant to hold children responsible for what they do, although we find it hard to draw boundaries here. Mental illness is often recognized as an excuse. Some people are excused on the grounds of 'irresistible impulse'. (But there is still the problem, discussed by the Victorian judge Fitzjames Stephen and by many lawyers since, of distinguishing between irresistible impulses and those that simply were not resisted.) Also, where there is a fairly complete causal explanation of a person's action, there is sometimes less inclination to hold him responsible for it. Not only is there disagreement as to which of these excuses

---

1 This point is made by Professor H. L. A. Hart in his thorough discussion of the various uses of the word 'responsible': 'Varieties of Responsibility', *Law Quarterly Review*, 1967, reprinted in his *Punishment and Responsibility*, 1968. Cf. also Feinberg: 'Action and Responsibility', in Black (ed.), *Philosophy in America*, 1965.

should be recognized, but there is also the added complication that the excuses we accept vary with the gravity of the 'offence'. Aristotle thought that nothing would excuse matricide; J. L. Austin pointed out that 'I did it inadvertently' will do as an excuse for treading on a snail, but not for treading on the baby.

Examination of the accounts of responsibility proposed by Aristotle and Bradley has brought out the importance of moral attitudes in deciding where the boundaries of responsibility lie. Some of the disagreements between them are disputes about when to blame or punish, and result from different views about how men should be treated in various situations, rather than from any differences over concepts. It will be argued that this point is crucial for the solution to the problem of determinism and free will. Just as legal systems vary in deciding who should be punished, so people may vary in deciding who deserves praise or blame. Our attitudes towards people and what they do are influenced by our knowledge of them and their situation. But we are not forced by any facts, even the truth of determinism, to modify our attitudes. It is up to us to choose which considerations to accept as excuses or mitigation.

2

DETERMINISM

There is almost universal agreement among contemporary philosophers that we need no longer worry about determinism. We are assured that determinism is unintelligible, or that, although intelligible, it is an empty doctrine with no factual content, or that it is demonstrably false. And, for anyone still troubled after all these reassurances and refutations, there is the doctrine that, even if determinism is true, it is either compatible with, or presupposed by, all our ordinary beliefs about people and what they do. Perhaps an explanation should be given by anyone proposing to add to the vast literature devoted to a doctrine that is harmless in so many different ways. This chapter is a defence of the view that determinism is a perfectly intelligible empirical theory that may very well be true, and the next chapter suggests that it is a theory that raises serious problems of justifying some common beliefs about responsibility.

1 WHAT IS DETERMINISM?

Determinism, as defined here, is the thesis that all human behaviour is governed by causal laws. This view has in the past found supporters to claim that it was certainly true, perhaps because they held it to be entailed by some other allegedly indubitable principle such as 'every event has a cause'. It will be argued here, not that the determinist thesis is certainly true, but that it is an empirical hypothesis that we have no grounds for rejecting.

Determinism

Some philosophers[1] say that they do not know what the thesis of determinism is. And it is suggested that this is not so much because several different theses may bear the name 'determinism', but rather that any such thesis as the one defined here is in itself obscure. This obscurity can presumably be dispelled if it can be shown that determinism is a testable theory, and if some indication of what tests would be relevant can be given.

It is sometimes objected that determinism is not a genuinely testable theory because nothing would ever be allowed to prove it false.[2] The view that all human behaviour is governed by causal laws could only be refuted by showing that something someone does is uncaused. But if there were an apparently uncaused event of this kind, a convinced determinist could refuse to accept that it really was uncaused. There is always the possibility of there being some cause as yet undiscovered. Since one can never with certainty identify an uncaused event, determinism is strictly unfalsifiable, and hence, it is argued, vacuous.

But while it must be admitted that determinism is unfalsifiable, this does not entail either that it is untestable or that it is vacuous. There is a common view, originally and most explicitly argued for by Professor Popper,[3] that all empirical statements must be falsifiable. Popper holds that we can never conclusively verify any strictly universal empirical law, on the grounds that, while all the experiments so far conducted may support it, we cannot be sure that this will continue to be so in future. Thus verifiability cannot be the defining characteristic of empirical statements. But a single instance can be sufficient to falsify a general law: the discovery of one black swan adequately refutes the statement that all swans are white. Popper therefore proposes that we should make falsifiability the criterion of whether or not a statement is empirical. One disadvantage of this convention is that it forces Popper to classify any existential statement without some spatio-temporal reference (e.g. 'Black ravens exist') as 'non-empirical or metaphysical', since nothing would ever count as

1 E.g. Professor P. F. Strawson, 'Freedom and Resentment', *Proceedings of the British Academy*, 1962, p. 127.
2 Cf. G. J. Warnock, 'Every Event has a Cause', in Flew, *Logic and Language* (Second Series), 1953. This view was earlier adopted by Professor Popper, *The Logic of Scientific Discovery*, 1959, p. 61 (English edition of his previous *Logik der Forschung*).
3 *Op. cit.*, Chs. 1, 3 and 4.

falsifying such a statement. This oddity can be avoided, without begging any questions about whether future evidence will force us to reject beliefs we hold on the basis of present or past evidence, by a modification of Popper's convention. If we abandon the demand that all empirical statements must be falsifiable, and substitute for it the more liberal demand that all empirical statements must be testable (i.e. either verifiable or falsifiable) we can avoid the paradoxical view that 'black ravens exist' is a metaphysical statement. Since it can be verified by a single instance, it is an empirical statement, and can be distinguished from those existential statements (e.g. 'There exist numbers, as well as numerals') that really are metaphysical, in that no evidence will ever count for or against them.

One consequence of this modification is that it is no longer clear that determinism is untestable. It can be argued that determinism, although unfalsifiable, is a doctrine that could in principle be verified and is thus still an empirical thesis. But this can only be made plausible if some account is given of what it would be to verify the determinist thesis. The account that is relevant here is suggested by consideration of a similar thesis about a computer. If we discovered a computer whose internal workings were unknown to us, we might wonder whether or not its operations were governed by any discoverable causal laws. We would investigate this by trying to correlate different types of input with different types of output, constructing generalizations of the form 'Feeding in data x together with instructions y is always followed by output z.' We might or might not supplement such generalization by further correlations of both input and output with different internal states of the machine. And, when all the performance so far observed had been brought under such generalizations, it would be necessary to test them by deriving predictions about the machine's future performance. Consistently correct predictions would count as verifying the hypothesis that the machine was governed by the causal laws in question.[1]

---

1 The hypothesis is only verified, strictly speaking, when it is the *simplest* hypothesis to give the greatest power of successful prediction. It is notoriously true that logically incompatible theories can generate identical predictions. Although the notion of simplicity must be invoked here to explain how determinism is verifiable, I shall not attempt the difficult task of analysing this concept.

This computer example suggests how we could verify the determinist thesis. We can only do this by constructing causal laws that both account for all the data already available and entail testable statements about instances not at present known to us. This second condition makes it necessary that our causal laws will be able to account for human actions, performed either now or in the past, of which we are ignorant at the time of constructing our generalizations, and that the laws will enable us to make correct predictions about future actions. Verification of the thesis would entail that each future action of any particular person could in principle be predicted. To show that determinism was true would involve discovering causal laws sufficiently comprehensive to cover all the behaviour of any given person through any given stretch of time. Each of these causal laws will, on Popper's view, be falsifiable rather than verifiable, and yet taken together they will count as verifying the unfalsifiable thesis of determinism. This may seem paradoxical, and it may be objected that one cannot verify a hypothesis by providing other hypotheses that cannot themselves be verified. But this objection can be met by pointing out that the unverifiable hypotheses are only unverifiable in the sense in which, according to Popper, all strictly universal empirical laws are unverifiable. This objection is a concealed form of the objection to inductive argument in general: it is no more and no less of a difficulty for the determinist thesis than for other empirical statements such as 'the performance of this machine is governed by causal laws'.

It is, of course, open to a critic to point out that the determinist thesis cannot either be verified conclusively or falsified conclusively. Popper admits universal statements to the realm of empirical discourse on the grounds that a single repeatable experiment can falsify them conclusively, and the argument for admitting existential statements rests on the possibility of them being conclusively verified by a single confirming instance. But again, this objection to determinism can be shown to be one that holds against any universal empirical generalization. Just as such generalizations can never, for the reason Popper gives, be verified beyond all possible doubt, so, for the same reason, they can never be falsified beyond all possible doubt. Popper's position depends on a form of selective philosophical scepticism, that involves taking doubts about the future seriously, while ignoring doubts about the past. It is always possible for us to doubt that the falsifying instance really occurred, on the grounds of a general scepticism about the reliability of memory or of any evidence about the past. And even if the generalization did not hold good in the past, we cannot, on Popper's view, be sure that it will not start to hold from now on. I do not wish to defend these extreme forms of scepticism, but only to point out that there is no reason why they should be taken less seriously than Popper's scepticism about whether future evidence will confirm the beliefs we base on past evidence. That our memories of falsifying experiments do not deceive us cannot be demonstrated beyond all possible doubt, but we can surely have enough evidence to put it beyond all reasonable doubt. That well supported general laws such as the determinist thesis might become will continue to hold in the future cannot be demonstrated beyond all possible doubt, but we can surely have enough evidence to put it beyond all reasonable doubt. The determinist thesis shares with all universal empirical generalizations the feature that is always possible, but not always reasonable, to ask both whether it is really true and whether it is really false. That it has this feature does nothing to remove its status as an empirical theory.

Another objection sometimes raised against the view that determinism is a testable theory is that, when we make our predictions of future human actions, we can never be sure that we have considered all the relevant factors. But this again is not a difficulty peculiar to determinism: it can be raised with equal force against any empirical theory. Whenever we make predictions of any kind, it is always logically possible that we have overlooked some factor which will influence events in such a way as to falsify our predictions. The reason why this is not an important difficulty in well established practical sciences, such as engineering, is that we know on the basis of long experience which considerations will in fact prove relevant when we are predicting. There seems no reason why accumulated experience should not give us the same sort of practical knowledge in psychology and the other human sciences. If this is admitted, the logical possibility of ignoring some factor relevant to a prediction loses its importance. The argument that determinism is testable is not weakened by showing that determinism shares the limitations of all testable theories.

2 PREDICTABILITY

To state what would count as proving determinism true is to give anti-determinists an opportunity to say that such conditions could not ever be satisfied. Determinism entails that all human behaviour is predictable, and many philosophers say that this is demonstrably false. Professor Hampshire[1] has drawn attention to an important difficulty in predicting human behaviour. If a man is faced with a choice between two courses of action, it may be possible to predict the outcome of his choice. But, if he learns of the prediction, this knowledge may influence him in such a way as to falsify the prediction. And a higher-order prediction, taking the effect of the first prediction into account, will run into the same difficulty unless it is concealed from the person choosing. The claim that a man's behaviour is completely and publicly predictable gives rise to an infinite regress. If complete public predictions cannot be made in practice, the claim that they can be made 'in principle' is an empty one.

There are other similar infinite regress arguments against total predictability. It is sometimes said that the making of each pre-diction would itself have to be predicted, and that this could lead to an infinite regress. This argument shows that we cannot predict every event, but this should not be confused with the view that there are some events that cannot be predicted. It is easy to see the possibility of an infinitely long sentence: a pre-diction of a prediction of a prediction . . . and so on. This only shows that predictions could be infinitely long, not that they must be. One can always terminate one's prediction, and where one chooses to do so is entirely a matter of convenience. It is true that, after the point at which I choose to stop, there will remain events as yet unpredicted, but this will in any case be true if there is an infinite number of future events of any kind. Because there are infinitely many future events, I cannot predict

1 *Thought and Action*, 1959, Ch. 2. It is not clear that Hampshire himself sees his argument as an anti-determinist one. He has elsewhere rejected the attempt to provide *a priori* arguments in support of the claim that some events cannot be scientifically explained. Cf. 'Freedom of Mind', The Lindley Lecture, University of Kansas, 1965, p. 13. For discussion of the question of the predictability of one's own decisions, cf. Pears, 'Predicting and Deciding', *Proceedings of the British Academy*, 1964.

them all in one finitely long sentence, but it does not follow from this that there is any one future event that cannot be predicted.

Professor Popper has an argument concerning the unpredictability of new ideas and hence of actions influenced by them. He says that 'if there is such a thing as growing human knowledge, then we cannot anticipate today what we shall know only tomorrow'.[1] Here there is a confusion between what we can predict and what we do predict. The suggestion is that, if a new idea or discovery is predictable, it is no longer new when it occurs. It is true that if today I predict what your idea tomorrow will be, then I have already had the idea and you can claim no originality. But new ideas could still be produced even if all human behaviour was predictable, because it would not follow from this that all human behaviour was predicted.

Another argument of Popper's[2] is that in classical physics there are limitations on our powers of prediction similar to the more publicized limits found in quantum physics. He argues for this by considering the limitations of a mechanical predictor. A machine able to make predictions about the world can never fully predict every one of its own future states, and hence cannot predict the future of the environment with which it interacts. This can be illustrated by an example suggested by Professor Scriven.[3] He describes a computer with 'total data' and unbounded speed, connected to a photo-electric cell and a lamp. It is programmed to predict whether the lamp will be alight five minutes later. The photo-electric cell is focused on the output tape, and the lamp connected so that the answer 'yes' switches it off, and 'no' switches it on. The prediction is thus self-invalidating.

Popper's argument raises the same difficulties for a determinist view of computers that Hampshire's argument raises for a determinist view of men. Both can be met in the same way. Hampshire's argument can only be used to refute a version of the determinist thesis that sets a needlessly high standard of publicity for the predictions by which it is tested. To demonstrate that one could predict someone's future behaviour, it would be quite

---

1 *The Poverty of Historicism*, 1957 (from the Preface).
2 'Indeterminism in Classical and Quantum Physics', *British Journal for the Philosophy of Science*, 1950.
3 'The Compleat Robot: A Prolegomena to Androidology', in Hook (ed.), *Dimensions of Mind*, 1960.

sufficient to write down the predictions and put them in a sealed box, to be opened after the predicted events had taken place. Predictions can be publicly tested without being publicly made. Admittedly, one could not be sure of avoiding infinite regress when predicting the outcome of one's own choices, but verification of the determinist thesis only demands that everyone's behaviour can be predicted by somebody, not necessarily by himself. Similarly, while Popper's predictor may not be able to predict its future states, there is no reason why those states should not be predicted by some other machine. The two conditions that must be satisfied are that two such machines cannot each be used to predict the future states of the other, and that the machine making the predictions must not be allowed to influence the environment of the other one. This type of argument does not undermine determinism in man or machine.

3 IS MAN A MACHINE?

The doctrine of mechanism, that man is a machine, is almost as unclear as it is unpopular. Determinism is widely held to entail that men are no different from machines, since it makes the behaviour of men as predictable as the performance of machines. But predictability is not the only characteristic of machines. When we think of machines, we tend to think of them as unconscious, as made of inorganic material, and as manufactured by human beings. Yet it is not clear that any one of these features is necessary. When writers of science fiction describe conscious machines, it is not obvious that they are contradicting themselves. Machines such as spinning-wheels can be made of organic material such as wood. The requirement that a machine be manufactured by human beings is obscure: as Scriven[1] has asked, does a mother 'manufacture' her baby? Certainly determinism in no way entails that men are unconscious, inorganic, or 'manufactured' in any very surprising way. But the determinist doctrine that men exhibit causal regularities just as much as machines does suggests that machines might be constructed to exhibit the same causal regularities as men, perfectly reproducing human beha-

1 'The Compleat Robot: A Prolegomena to Androidology', in Hook (ed.), *Dimensions of Mind,* 1960.

viour. If mechanism is simply the doctrine that human behaviour is a mechanical performance in the sense that it could be reproduced by a machine, then determinism leaves the truth or otherwise of this doctrine as an open empirical question. Determinism undermines the view that there is any logical barrier in the way of this programme.

The widespread desire to find a logical gulf between men and machines is partly the result of an excessive concentration, both by mechanists and their opponents, on very simple mechanical processes. Pascal said that 'the calculating machine produces effects which are closer to thought than to anything that animals do; but it does nothing which can lead one to say that it has a will, as animals have'. In the seventeenth century it was legitimate for Pascal, as the designer of a calculating machine, to take this view. Philosophers adopting similar positions in the twentieth century should have their attention directed to the mechanisms of self-guiding missiles or of Deutsch's 'machine with insight'.[1] Hostility to mechanism might be reduced if psychologists did not so often produce crude models to explain sophisticated processes. The view that conscience is a 'conditioned reflex' is a case in point. A theory such as this, which appears to deny the possibility of moral action being either spontaneous or rational, is thought of as 'mechanistic'. But the objection to this type of theory is not that it explains conscience in terms of some mechanism, but rather than the explanation is in terms of a mechanism manifestly too crude to produce the sophisticated behaviour in question. If men are machines, they are machines that can do all that man can do: a truism that should both reassure philosophers and provide a standard by which to judge the mechanisms of psychological theory.

A very proper rejection of crude mechanisms proposed by psychologists too often leads philosophers to produce invalid arguments 'refuting' the general thesis that man is a machine. One of the best known of such arguments is that of Professor Ryle.[2] He argues that the fear that everything can be explained by mechanical laws is baseless, because such a fear is unintelligible. He likens the laws of physics to the rules of chess, and says that physical laws do not limit our freedom any more than fixed rules

1 *The Structural Basis of Behaviour,* 1960, Ch. 10.
2 *The Concept of Mind,* 1949, Ch. 3.

limit the chess player's freedom. He reminds us that strategies in chess are not 'reducible' to the rules.

But the parallel between physical laws and the rules of chess is not exact. The chess player is able, if playing against an un-observant opponent, to break the rules. We have not lost our freedom because its exercise is dishonourable. Yet we cannot dishonourably break the laws of physics. And, although strategies in chess are not reducible to the rules, they are still limited by them. To see this, one need only compare the number of strage-gies available to the chess player with the smaller choice open to someone playing within the less liberal rules of draughts. The view that men are as predictable as machines presupposes that the rules of physics are so strict that, in any given situation, they are in fact compatible with only one strategy. The alternative view that they leave open as many strategies as the rules of chess is one that must be argued for rather than merely asserted.

Another method of argument against the mechanist thesis is to cite specific human abilities that it is alleged no machine could duplicate. One such argument depends upon Gödel's theorem, and has been set out by Mr J. R. Lucas.[1] Gödel's theorem states that, in any consistent system strong enough to produce simple arithmetic, there are formulae that cannot be proved within the system, but which we can see to be true. Machines are what Lucas calls 'concrete instantiations of formal systems', and so Gödel's result applies to them. Thus, for any consistent machine that can do simple arithmetic, there is a 'Gödel statement' that we, but not the machine, can prove to be true. Lucas concludes that the human mind has at least one ability that a machine cannot have.

To sustain any sharp distinction between minds and machines, this argument would have to show that any human mind has some ability that no machine could duplicate. This it does not do. Lucas shows that each machine is incapable of proving its own Gödel statement. It is, of course, quite possible for one machine to prove the Gödel statement of another machine. It is even, Lucas admits, possible for a machine to develop more powerful techniques, so that it can prove the Gödel statement it previously found unprovable. But at this point, Lucas claims, it becomes a more powerful machine with a new, higher-order, Gödel statement.

[1] 'Minds, Machines and Gödel', *Philosophy*, 1961.

It must be conceded to Lucas that Gödel's theorem shows that any particular machine cannot prove its own Gödel statement, while a human being with sufficient mathematical competence could prove that particular Gödel statement. But this is an ability that a human being shares with any machine with sufficient mathematical competence, except the machine whose Gödel statement is in question. The interesting fact about a machine is that it cannot prove its own Gödel statement. To show that minds were superior in power to machines, Lucas would have to show that a human mind could prove its own Gödel statement. It is not clear that such an assertion is intelligible, but even if it is a coherent statement, it is not entailed by any of Lucas's arguments. And one can make the stronger point that to show that a human mind can prove its own Gödel statement entails admitting that it has one. It is hard to see how this could be admitted without conceding that a human being also is a 'concrete instantiation of a formal system', which is just what Lucas sets out to deny.

These difficulties in the anti-mechanist argument from Gödel's theorem are independent of any limitations on human powers that there may be in practice. Lucas could resist criticisms of his position based on human limitations that are practical rather than logical. Professor Putnam,[1] for example, says that, given a Turing machine T, I can find a proposition U such that I can prove

(A): 'If T is consistent, U is true'

where, if T is consistent, U is undecidable by T. But (A) can also be proved by T. Putnam says that although T, if consistent, cannot prove U, I cannot prove U either, unless I can prove that T is consistent, which is unlikely if T is very complicated. But the fact that a machine may be too complicated for me to be able to prove it consistent does not show that there is any logical barrier to my doing so. The relevant stage of Lucas's argument could be interpreted as saying that it is logically possible for me to prove both the consistency of T and the truth of (A), which taken together entail the truth of U, while it is not logically possible for T to do this. No practical difficulties raised by the complexity of T will be sufficient to refute this contention. But,

[1] 'Minds and Machines', in Hook, *op. cit.*

31

fortunately, the logical objections to Lucas's view, by impugning its consistency, make it unnecessary to rely on practical limitations of this kind.

The argument over the relevance of Gödel's theorem to the mechanist thesis can be paralleled with reference to other undecidability theorems. Scriven[1] mentions the Löwenheim–Skolem theorem in this connection. On his account, the Löwenheim–Skolem theorem shows that it is not possible to give a unique characterization of the real numbers, and hence of the irrational numbers, in that any attempted strict formalization of the real numbers can be shown to be ambiguous: it can be given at least one interpretation in the rational numbers. This means that every formalization can legitimately be interpreted in a way not intended, omitting any reference to the irrationals.

This theorem cannot be used any more successfully than Gödel's theorem to show that men have abilities that are in principle denied to machines. To prove this, one would have to show that ambiguous strict formalizations of the real numbers could be produced such that men could tell which interpretation was the intended one, while machines could not. If a situation were described in which men consistently interpreted the formalization correctly, while machines gave correct interpretations no more often than would be produced by chance, one of three kinds of explanation could be given. It might just be a long string of coincidences: this is empirically unlikely and logically uninteresting. Certainly such a situation could not count as evidence for any theory about the relative abilities of men and machines. Another explanation of the situation might be that men were able to interpret certain clues that were relevant from the context in which the formalization was proposed. But such an interpretation would be governed by rules, which could presumably be fed into an appropriately designed machine. The assertion that there are some rules which no machine could be designed to obey is unplausible (unless one counts rules that are self-contradictory or embody logical paradoxes) and one that certainly need not be accepted in the absence of supporting argument. The only remaining explanation would be that men simply had correct intuitions concerning the interpretation intended,

[1] *Op. cit.* Scriven rejects the use of the theorem as part of an argument against 'mechanism'.

while machines did not. It is a commonplace that to say one knows something by intuition is to give no explanation of how one knows it. The account of the situation in terms of a string of correct intuitions thus does not differ from the account in terms of a string of guesses that are correct by coincidence. None of these possible accounts of the situation entails any general conclusion about the respective logical possibilities open to men and machines.

The discussion of these anti-mechanist arguments has stressed that what machines cannot do, we cannot do either. One can give the same statement a different emphasis by saying that anything we can do, machines can do too. And this serves to remind us that when we speak here of what machines can do, we are speaking of what machines can in principle be constructed to do. It must be admitted that no machine at present in existence can reproduce all the behaviour of a man. But anti-mechanists are not simply making this platitudinous assertion; they argue that it is logically impossible to build a machine that could do so. These arguments have been challenged here. Yet it may be said that it is not sufficient for a mechanist to reject the particular arguments advanced against his view. As it is admitted that no existing machine can do all that a man can do, the mechanist is under some obligation to say (at least in outline) what sort of machine he has in mind. The position defended here is that there are no logical barriers in the way of determinism and mechanism: it is an open empirical question whether or not we will discover causal laws governing all human behaviour, and it is also an open empirical question whether or not, if we found such laws, we would have the ingenuity to design a machine with the same abilities that we have. In defending this view, one is not committed to advocating any particular method of research in the human sciences; nor is one committed in advance to any particular type of machine. But it is not irrelevant to mention that an 'inductive machine' of the kind outlined by Professor Smart,[1] capable of learning by observation the rules governing its own behaviour, would reproduce our capacity for proving an ascending series of higher-order Gödel statements.

[1] *Philosophy and Scientific Realism*, 1963, Ch. 6.

4 LIBERTARIAN ARGUMENTS FROM INTROSPECTION

There are philosophers who hold that some of our experiences give us grounds for supposing that some of our actions do not have causes. Professor Campbell,[1] speaking of our experience of 'moral effort', says, 'If we scrutinize that experience with care, we shall see that part and parcel of it is an indefeasible certitude that I "need not" be creating this rupture, and I could be acting otherwise, that there were genuinely "open possibilities" before me at the moment of volition.' Elsewhere Campbell refers to 'the contra-causal sort of freedom'. Mr W. F. R. Hardie[2] says that libertarians are committed to the doctrine of Free Will (the capital letters indicating a technical term used to refer to Campbell's 'contra-causal' freedom). Hardie says that libertarians hold that the Free Will doctrine 'correctly interprets a natural conviction', that 'its truth is a condition of moral obligation and moral responsibility', and that 'Free Will is a fact'. At this stage, the first and last of these three libertarian doctrines must be considered.

The first libertarian doctrine, that our experience of moral effort involves a conviction that we are at that moment not governed by causal laws, is hard to evaluate. All statements based on introspection are notoriously difficult to check. If one man says that moral efforts of will are always accompanied by the belief that they are uncaused, while another man denies this, it is not clear how their dispute can be resolved. It may be that what is true of one man's experience is false of that of another man. Or it may be that one man has 'overlooked' some feature of his inner experience, in a manner analogous to the way that we sometimes fail to notice something in our visual field. Some philosophers, influenced by Wittgenstein, maintain that statements purporting to be introspective reports are not evidence for anything at all, either because they are untestable or because it is not possible to make statements about private experiences in a language whose rules must be public. Whether or not these radical attacks on introspection are successful, one can legitimately doubt whether this question can be solved.

1 *Scepticism and Construction*, 1931, p. 131.
2 'My Own Free Will', *Philosophy*, 1957.

But considerations that, while not conclusive, are yet persuasive, can be brought both for and against this libertarian
doctrine. In defence of the doctrine, Hardie gives a number of
quotations from different philosophers to show that they accepted
it as true. When Sidgwick, Ross, Broad and Campbell all say
either that the doctrine is confirmed by their own introspection,
or else that the conviction of Free Will is presupposed in the
ordinary man's talk about responsibility, one wonders whether
widespread belief in a doctrine that people might be able to test
in their own case is not perhaps very strong evidence for its
truth. But against this one must set the fact that plausible accounts
have been given of why people might misdescribe their experience. Schopenhauer[1] suggests that people giving introspective
reports of efforts of will confuse the conviction that 'I can do
what I will' with the conviction 'I can will what I will'. One
might have a feeling of freedom when making an effort of will
because one knew that one could execute one's decision, and those
accustomed to contrasting free actions with caused actions
might misdescribe their feeling of freedom as a feeling that their
decision was uncaused. But, as has been admitted, these considerations are not conclusive, and since there are perhaps no
conclusive arguments here, the question must be regarded as still
open.

Even if we do have convictions of 'contra-causal' freedom, is
there any reason to suppose that these convictions are correct?
In the first place, it should be noted that such beliefs are in no way
self-guaranteeing. It is intelligible to speak of beings who mis-
takenly ascribed such freedom to themselves. Schopenhauer
brings this out when he imagines the water speaking to itself,
saying, 'I can make high waves . . . I can rush down hill . . . I
can boil away and disappear . . . but I am doing none of these
things now, and am voluntarily remaining quiet and clear water
in the reflecting pond.'[2] Similarly, Wittgenstein[3] imagined some
leaves blown about by the wind saying, 'Now I'll go this way . . .
now I'll go that way.' A less fanciful example of this is when a
man performs an action as the result of a post-hypnotic suggestion. In many cases he is unaware of the suggestion, and will
not include it among the causes of his decision to perform the

1 *Essay on the Freedom of the Will.*   2 *Ibid.*
3 Quoted in G. E. M. Anscombe, *Intention*, 1958.

action. But to an observer it may be obvious that the suggestion is the main cause of his decision to act as he does.

Both Hume[1] and Mill[2] give the same account of the libertarian's convictions of 'contra-causal' freedom. They suggest that a pre-Humean theory of causation leads people to think that their choices are uncaused because they are not conscious of any constraint upon them. They say that the libertarian belief is undermined as soon as it is seen that causation need not involve mysterious constraining bonds. If it were true that libertarianism rests on a pre-Humean view of causation, one could expect it to disappear if people came to accept the Humean view. It is not obvious that libertarianism does rest on a pre-Humean theory, but if Hume's account of causation is accepted in principle (with whatever detailed reservations one may have) the libertarian conviction is made to seem very odd indeed. As Professor Nowell-Smith[3] has argued, a statement that an action or an effort of will is not caused could only be established, if at all, by searching for causal regularities and not finding them. It is hard to see how any feeling of 'contra-causal' freedom could possibly establish that certain regularities were not to be found. Hardie replies to this argument by saying that the conviction of Free Will is not an object of introspection, but is discovered by self-scrutiny. I know what I am thinking by introspection, but I know what I think by self-scrutiny that need not involve introspection. But however I come to know what I think, there remains the question of how I can justify what I think. If I think that an event is not explicable in terms of causal regularities, the only justification I can have for my opinion is that I have made a thorough search for such regularities and failed to find them. And this brings us back to the argument being advanced here, that whether or not all human behaviour is governed by causal laws is a matter for empirical investigation. Libertarians have certain convictions about the answer to this question, but these convictions do not themselves provide that answer.

At this stage of the argument, some clarification may be demanded of the question of the relation between the determinist thesis and various views about the relationship between mind and body. It is sometimes held that determinism fits well the

1 *Enquiry*, Section 8.   2 *System of Logic*, Book 6, Ch. 2.
3 'Determinists and Libertarians', *Mind*, 1954.

theory that mental processes are to be identified with brain processes, but that any kind of dualism causes difficulties for determinism. This is perhaps because the brain is often seen as a physical mechanism which is interfered with at crucial points by 'mental' forces such as 'volitions'. So distinguished a neurophysiologist as Eccles[1] has suggested that mental processes may intervene at the moment a neural impulse crosses a synapse, in such a way as to determine its direction after the synapse. But even if (incredibly) there were this kind of interaction between mind and brain this would not be incompatible with determinism. For a determinist, all human behaviour is subject to causal regularities. He need not specify whether the regularities are to be stated in terms of physical events, mental events, or both. Determinism is neutral with respect to the various proposed solutions to the mind-body problem. It neither asserts nor denies the existence of 'volitions': it only says that, if they do exist, they are caused.

5 ACTIONS AND MOVEMENTS

There is a widespread belief among philosophers that a sufficient explanation of a human action can never be given in causal terms. Professor Peters[2] has said that 'if we are in fact confronted with a case of a genuine action (i.e. an act of doing something as opposed to suffering something), then causal explanations are *ipso facto* inappropriate as sufficient explanations'. His argument for this view rests on the distinction between a physical movement and a human action. He says: 'In the mechanical conception of "cause" it is also demanded that there should be spatial and temporal contiguity between the movements involved. Now the trouble about giving this sort of explanation of human actions is that we can never specify an action exhaustively in terms of movements of the body or within the body. It is therefore impossible to state sufficient conditions in terms of antecedent movements which may vary concomitantly with subsequent movements.'

1 *The Neurophysiological Basis of Mind,* 1953 (in the final chapter).
2 *The Concept of Motivation,* 1958, Ch. I. Cf. also Hamlyn, 'Behaviour', *Philosophy,* 1953, and Melden, *Free Action,* 1961. For criticism of this view, cf. Fodor, *Psychological Explanation: An Introduction to the Philosophy of Psychology,* 1968, Ch. I.

The stage of Peters' argument that will be criticized here is the statement that 'we can never specify an action exhaustively in terms of movements of the body or within the body'. Peters says that no single set of physical movements is necessary for any particular action. The action of signing a contract can involve quite different sets of physical movements on different occasions. I may hold the pen in my left hand or in my right hand; I may even hold it between my toes. But this kind of example only shows that no single set of overt physical movements (such as movements of one's limbs) is necessary for a particular action. It does not succeed in ruling out the possibility that some particular set of events in the brain is necessary for a particular action.[1]

In the present state of knowledge of the physiology and chemistry of the brain, it is not possible to say with certainty that there is a one-to-one correlation between mental states and brain states, although studies involving electrical stimulation of the brain suggest that this may be so.[2] This is an empirical question, which it would be foolish of philosophers to try to 'settle' in advance of the evidence. It is thus premature to assert that we cannot exhaustively specify actions in terms of bodily movements, for we do not yet know whether or not there is a single set of physical events in the brain, specific to each type of action, without which such actions cannot be performed. Actions are specified in terms of social conventions, but there is no reason why knowledge of a social convention should not involve some identifiable state of the brain. If neurophysiological and biochemical research shows that the decision to perform a particular action is always associated with a particular set of events in the brain, we will be a long way further on the way to giving complete causal explanations of what people do. Going back to the parallel drawn between the study of man and the investigation of a computer of unknown mechanism, we will have reached the stage where we can identify the function of the inner components of the computer, and causal

1 Necessary, but not sufficient. The events in the brain may occur in cases where I try to perform the action, but fail as a result of factors external to me. The view that one can give causal explanations of actions by citing physiological mechanisms does not commit one to the absurd view that thes e explanations are complete without any reference to interaction with the environment.
2 For an account of suggestive pioneering work, cf. Penfield, *The Excitable Cortex in Conscious Man*, 1958.

explanations of our actions will have the same degree of adequacy as causal explanations have for the performance of present day computers. If anyone were still to contend that they were 'inappropriate as sufficient explanations', it would be reasonable to regard the standard required for 'sufficiency' as too high to be worth taking seriously.

A similar argument can be brought in defence of the view that beliefs can be causes of actions. It has been argued[1] that the relation between beliefs and actions is a logical one, and cannot therefore be a causal one. Human causality can only hold between separately identifiable events, and it is suggested that beliefs cannot be identified separately from actions. While it is true that we often decide what a person believes on the basis of how he acts, this is not the only evidence we can have. Often we accept a person's verbal report of what he believes, although, as has been admitted, there is always the possibility of this being false, either because of lying or because of self-deception. But, if neurophysiologists and neurochemists succeed in establishing one-to-one correlations between mental states and brain states, together with satisfactory devices for detecting states of the brain, we will have means of identifying beliefs independently of either actions or verbal reports. The denial that beliefs can cause actions makes the unwarranted assumption that these one-to-one correlations cannot be established.

Sometimes philosophers hostile to determinism do not argue for the view that no actions are caused, but only claim that rational actions are uncaused. This view was at one time held by Professor MacIntyre,[2] who defined 'rational behaviour' as behaviour that can be influenced by logically relevant considerations. He said that, if presenting a man with logically relevant consideration is both a sufficient and a necessary condition for changing his mind, then on this occasion the possibility of other sufficient conditions is excluded. He concluded that, if a man's behaviour is rational, it cannot be determined by the state of his glands or by any other antecedent causal factor: it cannot be the

1 By Professor MacIntyre: 'A Mistake about Causality in Social Science', in Laslett and Runciman, *Philosophy, Politics and Society* (Second Series), 1962.
2 'Determinism', *Mind*, 1957. But cf. MacIntyre's later views in 'The Antecedents of Action', in Williams and Montefiore, *British Analytical Philosophy*, 1966.

effect of a set of sufficient conditions operating independently of the agent's deliberation. MacIntyre took this to show that scientific discoveries can never show that rational behaviour is causally determined.

This argument depends on a definition of 'rational behaviour' such that no action could ever be considered rational. Presenting a man with logically relevant considerations is never by itself a sufficient condition for changing his mind. There are always other conditions that must be satisfied, that can only be overlooked because they always are satisfied under normal conditions. The man whose mind is to be changed must be in a position where he is able to change his mind: he must not be drugged or under hypnosis, and his brain must be working properly. Given that there are no abnormalities of this kind, it is then legitimate to talk of the presenting of reasons as a sufficient condition for changing a man's mind. This may seem a pedantic point, but it is important to notice that features of a situation so normal that one takes them for granted are necessary conditions of rational decision.

The other weakness of this argument is that it assumes that reasons cannot be causes. MacIntyre realized that this might provoke objections, and considered the objection that the giving of a reason is a physical event that may count as a cause. His reply was that, if determinists count reasons as causes, they reduce determinism to a tautology. He said that we can distinguish a giving of reasons that is causally effective from a giving of reasons that is rationally effective: you may act because of the passion in my voice as I give reasons, or else because of the reasons themselves. MacIntyre concluded that rational action is only causally determined if we count anything that has any influence on behaviour as a cause of behaviour, which in his view reduces determinism to a tautology.

The distinction between your acting because of the reasons I give and your acting because of the passion in my voice as I give them does not disappear when we say that reasons are causes. The distinction remains, but is redescribed as a distinction between two kinds of causal story. And the charge that to count all influences on behaviour as causal influences reduces determinism to a tautology has no substance. However we choose to describe 'influences' on behaviour, the thesis that all human behaviour exhibits causal regularities is still in doubt, just because there is much human behaviour where no such regularities have yet been discovered.

A powerful defence of the possibility of reasons have a causal influence on actions has been provided by Professor Davidson.[1] He points out that a person can have a reason for an action, and perform the action, and yet this reason not be the reason why he did it. Where an action is explained in terms of a reason, it is essential that the agent performed the action because he had the reason. And unless the relationship suggested by the linking word 'because' is left completely mysterious, it is hard to see how one can suppose it to be other than a causal one.

The view that reasons can be causes is the basis of the determinist reply to the argument that one could not consistently claim to know the truth of determinism, since determinism would entail that we arrived at our beliefs as the result of a causal process rather than a rational one.[2] Even if one made the over-generous concession that only beliefs adopted after rational consideration could count as knowledge, one could still defend determinism by rejecting the contrast between causal processes and rational ones.

6 THE DETERMINIST PROGRAMME

The argument so far in this chapter has of necessity been largely negative. One can only defend a thesis whose truth one admits is still in doubt by criticising arguments purporting to refute it. But it may be said that a discussion of determinism is rather insubstantial unless some indication is given of the form that the causal laws in question might take. It may also be suggested that causal generalizations of a trivial kind could be constructed to fit any sequence of events at all, so that determinism is a pointless thesis

---

1 'Actions, Reasons and Causes', *Journal of Philosophy,* 1963. Cf. also Pears, 'Are Reasons for Actions Causes?' in Stroll, *Epistemology,* 1967. Pears gives complex arguments in reply to other objections, not discussed here, to the thesis that reasons can be causes of actions. The thesis is also defended by Fodor, *op. cit.,* Ch. I.

2 This argument is found (e.g.) in Joseph, *Introduction to Logic,* 1906, and in Wootton, *Testament for Social Science,* 1950. An apparently similar argument is used by Kant in his *Fundamental Principles of the Metaphysic of Ethics* to support the claim that freedom must be presupposed as a property of the will of all rational beings.

unless more information is given about the laws it promises. This charge of triviality is met by the account of determinism proposed here, where the causal generalizations have to satisfy (admittedly unspecified) criteria of simplicity, and to entail testable statements about instances not already known to us. The exact nature of the causal laws governing human behaviour is not something that need be specified before one can assert that such laws may exist. But, to avoid the charge of insubstantiality, it is perhaps worth glancing at the kinds of laws the human sciences may be expected to provide.

One can make a distinction between 'tight-fitting' and 'loose-fitting' laws. A tight-fitting law is one that gives unequivocal and precise predictions about the behaviour of the individual units in terms of which the law is stated. Thus the laws of Newtonian mechanics are tight-fitting, since, with enough information about initial conditions, they alone are sufficient to give categorical predictions of a non-statistical kind about the movements of physical bodies. A loose-fitting law, on the other hand, either is only capable of giving statistical predictions about the behaviour of the units in terms of which it is stated, or else gives predictions of an even vaguer kind. Thus laws concerning the paths of electrons, being only statistical, are loose-fitting. And if one were to propose so loose a 'law' as the statement 'most English parents take an interest in the education of their children' that too would be loose-fitting.

Laws in the social sciences (economics, social anthropology, sociology, social psychology) seem unlikely very often to be of the tight-fitting kind where individual people are units in terms of which they are stated. Many social scientists do not consider that individuals are the units that should figure in their laws: their units are societies, social classes, towns, businesses, tribes and housing estates. And it is also true that some social scientists, notably many social anthropologists, do not consider the discovery of general laws to be part of their task. Where laws are proposed, they will perhaps sometimes entail predictions about the behaviour of individuals, but these will normally be statistical. If, for example, economists say that farmers will benefit as a result of a certain economic policy, this is compatible with a small number of individual farmers being bankrupted by it.

Where we are looking for concrete predictions about the

behaviour of a particular person, we will normally at least have to supplement the data of the social sciences by information derived from individual psychology. But here again the outlook is unpromising. In one psychological study, it was found that 13 per cent of students at Dartmouth College regularly had accompanying coloured visual images when they listened to music.[1] Could one use purely psychological laws to predict whether or not a particular person had such visual images? It is perhaps conceivable that psychology might one day reach such a peak of sophistication that we could with certainty make such a prediction, based on some statement like 'all endomorphic introverts coming from broken homes in South London, with I.Q. over 130, have coloured visual images when listening to music'. But this seems hardly plausible. It is surely more likely that for this type of prediction we should have to go to the physiology of the person's brain, and the general laws to which we should appeal would be those of neurophysiology rather than of psychology.[2] Or again, it seems unlikely that those features of an old person's behaviour that depend on the rate at which his mental powers decline could be predicted without reference to the state of his brain and to neurophysiological knowledge. Boyle's Law is a generalization about the behaviour of gases, while one needs the kinetic theory of gases to explain the mechanism underlying that behaviour. In Deutsch's[3] powerful image, the discoveries of neurophysiology may do for psychology what the kinetic theory did for Boyle's Law. This may have been what was meant by Freud, the most influential of all determinists, when he said that 'the deficiences in our description would probably vanish if we were already in a position to replace the psychological terms by physiological or chemical ones'.[4]

Determinists legitimately place great hopes in neurophysiology. But even here one should be cautious about speculating beyond the fragmentary evidence that we now have. It is possible that tight-fitting predictions of an individual person's behaviour might be derived from laws stated purely in terms of the firing of nerve cells, where the firing of each cell could be explained either by

---

1 Karwoski and Odbert, 'Colour-Music', *Psychological Monograph*, 1938.
2 Cf. the article by Mr B. A. Farrell in *British Journal of Psychology*, 1955.
3 *Op. cit.*, Ch. I.
4 *Beyond the Pleasure Principle*, translated by James Strachey, 1950, p. 54.

environmental stimulus or by the firing of some other nerve cell or group of nerve cells. And this belief may be reinforced by the powerful model now current of the brain as a computer. But it should be remembered that a model is only a model: Descartes was as fascinated by his model based on a hydraulic mechanism as the theorists at the beginning of our own century were by their model of the brain as a telephone exchange. These images, reflecting the technological developments of their times, should warn us against too confidently seeing in ourselves the reflection of our own machines. It is already clear that, even if the brain in some interesting ways functions like a computer, the small size but frequent occurrence of our mistakes in calculation far more closely resembles the type of error made by the neglected analogue computers than that of the digital computers which have captured our imaginations.[1]

While it is possible that the brain is a mechanism whose causal laws can be stated in purely physiological terms, it is equally possible that we will have to go down to the chemical level for an adequate causal account. There is no reason to be dogmatic one way or the other, but it is possible to indicate situations where chemical activity might bring about non-trivial events that were 'random' at the physiological level. Nerve impulses travelling along a neural pathway cross from one neuron to another at a synapse. Although in a very few cases this crossing of the synapse is simply a matter of electric current leaping the gap, in the vast majority of synapses studied a chemical mechanism is involved. A chemical transmitter, such as acetylcholine or noradrenaline, is released by the first neuron, crosses to the second one, and starts it firing. Although neurons sometimes fire 'randomly', the standard 'physiological' causal account of why a neuron fires is that it has been triggered off by the firing of one or more adjacent neurons. But it appears that small packets of the chemical transmitter are released across synapses all the time, when the pre-synaptic neuron is not carrying a nerve impulse.

> There is very strong evidence that the motor nerve terminals are, even 'at rest', in a state of intermittent 'secretory activity' and that they liberate small quantities of acetylcholine at random intervals at an average rate of about one per second.

1   Cf. J. Z. Young, *A Model of the Brain,* 1964, Ch. 3.

A nerve impulse causes this activity to become enormously intensified for a very brief moment so that a few hundred of these unitary events become synchronized within less than one milli-second.[1]

We cannot at present rule out the possibility that sometimes a neuron fires, not as the result of the firing of adjacent neurons, but as the result of summation of 'random' transmitter release from them. It may be that the 'random' firing of a single neuron has no influence on human behaviour, or it may be that random firing is never brought about by the random release of transmitter. But, until we have grounds for accepting either of these denials, we have at least one reason for wondering whether generalizations at the chemical level may not be needed to supplement any purely physiological account of the causal mechanisms of the brain.

This brings out a certain flexibility in the determinist position as outlined here. The determinist is not committed to the view that the causal laws governing human behaviour must be psychological, must be physiological, must be chemical or must be physical. All he claims is that there is some set of causal laws, at whatever level or levels of explanation, that entail tight-fitting predictions of human behaviour, and that there is no human behaviour that is in principle unpredictable on the basis of a knowledge of these laws and of the initial conditions in which they operate. For this reason, among others, a determinist need not be as worried by parts of quantum theory as some physicists have supposed.

It is said that Heisenberg has shown that the behaviour of elementary particles is not causally determined. Heisenberg's claim is that it is in principle impossible for us to measure with unlimited precision both the position and the momentum of a particle at the same time. We can measure its position only at the cost of interfering with its momentum, and measuring its momentum involves altering its position. When we know about the position we can assign a probability to its having a certain momentum, and vice versa. It is said that because we cannot talk with certainty of the simultaneous position and momentum of a particle, we have no right to talk of its having a causally determined path. (The stronger claim is that such talk would be

1 Katz, *Nerve, Muscle, and Synapse*, 1966, Ch. 9.

meaningless.)[1] The problem is complicated by the fact that talk about particles in this context is not wholly literal. Subatomic phenomena in some ways do and in other ways do not resemble particles in motion. But since the anti-determinist argument is stated in terms of the particle model, it seems legitimate to presuppose this model is indicating gaps in the argument. The most dubious assumption on which the argument rests is the belief that, if we are in principle unable to chart a particle's causally determined path, the claim that it has such a path must either be false or meaningless. The view that such a claim is meaningless presupposes a verification theory of meaning that has enormous, and as yet unresolved, difficulties. The view that such a claim must be false presupposes a philosophical prohibition on postulating unobservables, which, in order to be sustained, requires more argument in its defence than it has so far received.

But it must be admitted that, within the present conceptual scheme of subatomic physics, Heisenberg's results do present a serious challenge to the empirical status of any theory of determinism at subatomic level. The empirical status of determinist claims about human behaviour has been defended here by arguing that, although they are not falsifiable, such claims are in principle verifiable. But this line of defence could not be used on behalf of the empirical status of any determinist thesis about subatomic particles. For while, for reasons given earlier, any determinist thesis is unfalsifiable, Heisenberg's claims seem to show subatomic determinism to be also unverifiable. Without some conceptual revolution, at present hard to envisage, to make Heisenberg limitations irrelevant, it seems that we must accept that the view that elementary particles have causally determined paths is not empirical. It is not clear without further argument that this entails that the view is either non-factual or untrue. But its status would be very disturbing for the determinism defended in this chapter, if a determinist doctrine about human behaviour could be shown to depend upon determinism at the level of elementary particles.

1   Obscure versions of this argument are scattered throughout Bohr's two collections of papers: *Atomic Theory and the Description of Nature*, 1934, and *Atomic Physics and Human Knowledge*, 1958. Thorough and detailed criticism of this type of argument can be found in Nagel, *The Structure of Science*, 1961, Ch. 10.

However, the flexibility of the determinist position defended here gives a possible escape from this embarrassment. Just as causal 'gaps' at the physiological level might be filled in by going down to the chemical level, so a breakdown in causal explanation at subatomic level might be made harmless at a more macroscopic level of explanation. It may be that the mechanisms underlying human behaviour are such that it is unaffected by variations in the path of a single electron. The statistical regularities at subatomic level may be quite adequate as a basis for causal laws at a higher level, where the units in terms of which the laws were stated would be unaffected in their behaviour by 'random' motions of subatomic particles. Again, one cannot be certain that this is so: it is an open empirical question. But it is important that the determinist thesis advanced here cannot be refuted merely by showing that some piece of behaviour is 'random' at one level of explanation, even if that level is the most microscopic.

To dwell on the variety of explanatory levels at which causal laws underlying human behaviour might be found is to see the boldness of any claim to have discovered an uncaused piece of it. It has been suggested that the selective direction of attention is a plausible candidate for the libertarian role of uncaused human event.[1] But it is hard to see what this plausibility comes to. Leaving aside the logical impossibility of *proving* any event to be uncaused, one can imagine what might make such a claim seem plausible. If science had reached such a stage that the social sciences, as well as psychology, physiology, biochemistry and physics, were all held to be 'complete', with no further causal laws to be discovered, one might then feel that an event which stubbornly resisted causal explanation at any level could plausibly be thought to be uncaused. Even this would perhaps be rash. But, at present, our knowledge is so far from this that one can only admire the daring of those who claim it already plausible that an event cannot be explained at any level. To show that psychological laws could not enable one to predict a switch of attention, or to show that there is a logical gulf between actions, beliefs and reasons on the one hand, and physical movements and causes on the other (even if either of these could be done), would only be to complete a fraction of the anti-determinist programme. Determinism not only cannot be proved false, but also

1 Cf. Franklin, *Freewill and Determinism,* 1968, Ch. 4.

cannot even be made unplausible by showing that at a single level of discourse it cannot be proved true.

A final point, worth making for its relevance to moral responsibility, is that our present uncertainty as to whether determinism is true is of little help to the libertarian. For, however great the difficulty of proving that all human behaviour is governed by causal laws, it is quite impossible to prove that any particular piece of behaviour is not causally determined. And if, in the absence of proof, the libertarian just chooses an act to call 'uncaused', and hopes for the best, there is always the danger that, even in the absence of satisfactory evidence for determinism in general, the libertarian's chosen act may still be causally explained. Scientific advance may undermine many varieties of libertarianism even before determinism is, if ever, proved true. Determinism may not be true, but the argument of this chapter has been that we have no good reasons for supposing it to be false.

3

EXCUSES

We have seen that to hold someone responsible for an action of his can be to hold that it is legitimate to praise, blame, reward or punish him for that action, where any of these responses would normally be appropriate. We have seen that some features of a case are generally held to eliminate or reduce a person's responsibility for what he does. It is suggested that we have no good grounds for supposing determinism false. Many philosophers have been convinced that determinism is incompatible with the possibility of people being responsible for what they do. The arguments for this view take many forms, but perhaps the most persuasive involves the contention that determinism entails that no one ever can act any differently from how he does act.

The argument can be stated as follows: I am only responsible for an action when I could have acted otherwise. If a correct prediction of how I would act was entailed by a set of true causal laws, together with statements of the initial conditions relevant to the operation of the laws in the particular circumstances, then I could not have acted otherwise. This is because my acting otherwise would have falsified one or more of the causal laws, but, *ex hypothesi,* all the causal laws are true. Since the existence of causal laws governing my action entails that I could not have acted otherwise, it entails that I was not responsible for my action. So the determinist thesis rules out the possibility of anyone ever being responsible for any action.

Arguments of this sort provide those who accept them with a

powerful motive for attempting to prove that determinism cannot be true. But some philosophers have wished to retain both moral responsibility and the possibility that determinism is true. The philosophers of the empiricist tradition, with remarkable uniformity,[1] have argued that the belief that determinism is incompatible with responsibility is confused and false. In this chapter I shall examine one classic statement of this reconciliationist view, together with one hostile reply. I shall go on in the next chapter to suggest that the conciliatory doctrine that determinism raises no problems for our normal beliefs about responsibility is false, but that we need not refuse ever to hold anyone responsible for what he does.

1 THE VIEWS OF SCHLICK AND CAMPBELL

Schlick[2] is concerned to provide an account of responsibility that allows us to hold some people responsible for some actions without committing us to the view that the determinist thesis is false. Like Bradley, Schlick holds that the central feature of our concept of responsibility is its intimate connection with reward and punishment. He says that the only point of asking if a man is responsible for an action is that we want to know whether or not to give him punishment (or, in other cases, reward). He rejects the view that the function of punishment is retributive, a view which he says 'ought no longer to be defended in cultivated society; for the opinion that an increase in sorrow can be "made good again" by further sorrow is altogether barbarous'. Schlick says that the purpose of punishment is to reform the criminal and to deter others from committing crimes. So, in assigning responsibility we are not concerned with 'remote causes' (as when a man has perhaps inherited his character from his great-grandparents); we are concerned only with deciding which people can effectively be punished or rewarded. On Schlick's

1 Almost identical versions of this doctrine are to be found in Hobbes, Hume, Mill, Russell, Schlick and Ayer. It can also be found (in the context of a discussion of divine foreknowledge) in St Augustine's *City of God*, Book 5. Sir Isaiah Berlin (in the Introduction to his *Four Essays on Liberty*, 1969) says the doctrine was originally formulated by the Stoic sage Chrysippus.
2 *Problems of Ethics,* translated by David Rynin, 1939, Ch. 7.

account, a man is responsible for his act if his motives for performing it can be influenced favourably by reward or punishment. And Schlick holds that this entails that a man acting under compulsion is not responsible for his action, but does not entail anything of the kind about a man whose action is governed by causal laws. He draws a sharp distinction between the laws of a state, which a man may be compelled to obey, and causal laws, which are merely generalizations about what happens, and which do not compel anything at all.

Schlick's account of responsibility has been criticized by Professor Campbell,[1] who, as a libertarian, holds both that some of our actions are uncaused and that this is presupposed by the way in which we decide when to hold people responsible. He argues that Schlick's account of responsibility ignores some important features of our normal use of the concept. For example, we do not normally hold animals responsible for their actions, and yet their future behaviour can be influenced favourably by reward and punishment. Similarly, Campbell argues, we may use sanctions to restrain a well-meaning but dangerous person, without necessarily holding him responsible for what he does. Campbell's criticisms of Schlick are not confined to arguing that there are people who would not normally be held responsible, but whom Schlick would have to hold responsible; he also says that Schlick's account is inconsistent with our normal willingness to hold dead men responsible for states of affairs which they brought about.

Some of Campbell's points are perhaps less powerful than he takes them to be. It is not clear, for example, that there is universal agreement that animals cannot be held responsible for their actions. Although it may be regarded as inhumane to administer punishment of a purely retributive kind to an animal, it is not uncommon for people to reward an animal for some piece of good behaviour, simply because they think the reward deserved, and without any intention of modifying the animal's future behaviour. And Campbell's argument that we hold dead people responsible for states of affairs is not seriously damaging to Schlick's view. Schlick could perhaps claim that here we are using 'responsible' in a different sense: Schopenhauer pointed

1 'Is "Free Will" a Pseudo-Problem?', *Mind*, 1951. Reprinted in his *In Defence of Free Will*, 1967.

out that sometimes we use 'he was responsible for the situation' merely to mean 'he caused the situation'. This is different from the sense of 'responsible' under discussion, for it entails nothing about the person's blameworthiness: he might have caused the situation by having a heart attack. Or, even if Schlick did not adopt this defence, he could save his theory by a minor modification. He could claim that, when we hold a character in history responsible for some state of affairs, we are asserting that his behaviour could have been favourably influenced by reward or punishment had it been applied at the time.

Campbell's most powerful argument is that we can apply sanctions to a well-meaning but dangerous person without holding him responsible for his actions. This example does establish that Schlick's use of 'responsible' diverges from its normal use, and a major modification of Schlick's theory would be necessary to close the gap between it and the popular view. And there is another such gap overlooked by Schlick, which he might find even more disturbing than that pointed out by Campbell. Schlick says that the point of punishment is to reform or deter. Having said this he discusses punishment purely in terms of reforming the criminal, to the neglect of its deterrent aspect. In this way, he overlooks the possibility that the punishment of an innocent man might have a deterrent effect, provided that the innocent man was generally believed to be guilty. (And it is even possible that it might have some deterrent effect where he was known to be innocent.) On purely utilitarian grounds, we might think an innocent man a fit subject for punishment. If, as on Schlick's view, the question 'Who is responsible?' is identified with the question 'Who should be punished?', we could be committed to saying that an innocent man is responsible for someone else's crime. Schlick only avoids this paradox by ignoring deterrence, so that he is able to treat 'Who is to be punished?' as if it were the same question as 'Whose motives must be altered to prevent repetition of the act?'

Another strong argument used by Campbell against Schlick is that often we are less inclined to hold someone fully responsible for an action where we believe that special features of his heredity or upbringing were important causal factors. This attitude is not universal, but many people would allow that 'he comes from a broken home', or 'he has an extra Y chromosome', is relevant to the assessment of a young man's responsibility for a crime. Schlick's account does not allow for this type of plea. But Campbell's account is equally inadequate as a description of common practice. Under the M'Naghten Rules, a man was held legally responsible for his actions unless he was 'labouring under such a defect of reason, from disease of the mind, as not to know the nature and quality of the act that he was doing, or, if he did know it, that he did not know he was doing what was wrong'. It would be unwise to assume that the M'Naghten Rules accurately reflected the plain man's view of moral responsibility, especially as they were frequently criticized as an unsuitable basis even for legal responsibility. While most people would probably approve of the rules following Bradley rather than Aristotle in allowing ignorance of right and wrong as an excuse, there has always been widespread criticism of their vagueness and of their stress on the criminal's knowledge rather than on his will power. But it is noticeable that these rules allow only one type of causal factor ('defect of reason', whatever that may be) to absolve from responsibility. And, although there is much criticism of the rules, this has normally taken the form of arguments for allowing other particular causal factors, such as 'irresistible impulses', to absolve from responsibility. The popular attitude to legal responsibility certainly does not seem to be that people should be absolved from such responsibility whenever we discover that their actions have any kind of cause at all. And this also holds for moral responsibility. If a man rapes a girl, we would perhaps normally hold him morally responsible for this, although our knowledge of the mechanics of sexual desire makes it possible to give the the outlines of a causal account of his action. Campbell says that libertarians need only claim 'contra-causal' freedom for the few cases where strongest desire clashes with duty. But one might feel that rape could normally be causally explained in terms of strongest desires defeating duty, and this explanation would not itself, as Campbell seems to suggest, automatically absolve a man from moral responsibility.

Neither Schlick nor Campbell has done justice to all the attitudes that underly our decisions about whether or not to hold people responsible in particular cases. Schlick cannot account for occasions when we use the word 'responsible' in some of the ways Campbell describes, while Campbell himself cannot account for uses of the word that seem quite compatible with the determinist thesis. It may be that some or all of us are confused and inconsistent in our criteria for ascribing responsibility, with the result that some decisions about responsibility presuppose that determinism is false while others do not. Or perhaps some people use one set of criteria while others use a different one. It is worth looking again at the sorts of excuses that often are allowed, to see if there are any general principles underlying them.

2 EXCUSES AND THEIR CLASSIFICATION

Aristotle said that we can only be praised or blamed for voluntary actions, which include all actions except those done in ignorance under compulsion. He gave no explanation of why we should accept the limitations imposed on praise and blame by this principle. Why should we accept ignorance and compulsion as the two kinds of excuse that we recognize?

A list of pleas that can be advanced to 'reduce' a statement like 'Smith hit her' has been drawn up by Professor Hart,[1] and these pleas are remarkably similar to those allowed by Aristotle. The list is as follows:

1 'Accidentally' (she got in the way while he was hammering in a nail).
2 'Inadvertently' (in the course of hammering in a nail, not looking at what he was doing).
3 'By mistake for someone else' (he thought she was May, who had hit him).
4 'In self-defence' (she was about to hit him with a hammer).
5 'Under great provocation' (she had just thrown the ink over him).
6 'But he was forced to by a bully' (Jones said he would thrash him).
7 'But he is mad, poor man.'

On this list, 'inadvertently', 'by mistake for someone else' and 'but he was forced to by a bully' are all excuses familiar to Aristotle. 'But he is mad, poor man' is an excuse Aristotle

---

1 'The Ascription of Responsibility and Rights', *Proceedings of the Aristotelian Society, 1948–9*; reprinted in Flew, *Logic and Language* (1st series), 1951.

would only allow provided that 'mad' is interpreted in the narrow intellectualist sense of the M'Naghten Rules. (The possibility of mental illness that destroys willpower, while leaving one's intelligence and moral sense unimpaired, was not allowed as an excuse by Aristotle, and raises special difficulties to be considered later.) Hart allows the excuse that an action was accidental, for which Aristotle makes no explicit provision. Hart's example, of a man who accidentally hits a woman while hammering in a nail, would probably be classified by Aristotle, together with cases of inadvertence, under the heading of 'ignorance of the nature of one's action'.

Of the pleas allowed by Hart, the only ones that clearly could not be included under Aristotle's headings of 'ignorance' and 'compulsion' are self-defence and provocation.[1] Many people would separate these two pleas from the others on Hart's list on the ground that these two are not excuses, but claims that an action is justified. There is an important distinction between justification and excuse, in that it is not the same to regard an action as justified (and hence not wrong) as it is to consider it wrong but excusable. But the existence of such a distinction does not mean that there is, in the case of any particular plea, a morally neutral test by which we can tell whether it is a justification or whether it is an excuse. The attitude a person adopts will depend on his moral beliefs. A pacifist might say of a man who fought in the Second World War that his action was wrong, but was excusable in view of the threat of Nazism, while a non-pacifist might say that to fight in such a war needs no excuse since it can be justified. Such a dispute cannot be resolved without discussing the question of what, if anything, justifies men participating in a war, and it is clear that to this question there are no morally neutral answers.

It may be that Aristotle would allow self-defence and provocation to count as justifications rather than excuses, and thus did not include them in his list of conditions that make an act involuntary.[2] If so, this rests on the moral belief that when one is acting in self-defence or under provocation it is not wrong to

---

1 Professor R. M. Hare has drawn my attention to what Aristotle does say about provocation: cf. *Nicomachean Ethics*, Book 5, Ch. 8.
2 This is plausible, for justified acts of self-defence are not normally involuntary.

do what would otherwise be a wicked act. The alternative is that Aristotle would not accept either plea as a justification or as an excuse. If this is so, it may just be that Hart is more lenient than Aristotle (who allows defence of one's family as some kind of mitigating factor). Perhaps if Aristotle had a category of 'diminished responsibility', he too would allow self-defence and provocation as factors 'reducing' a wicked act. If Hart and Aristotle disagree, Hart's account is reflecting features of how many people nowadays do think of responsibility, for people commonly do take a lenient view of actions done in self-defence or under provocation, even if they do not always allow these pleas to count as a complete justification or as a complete excuse.

But it is the similarity of the pleas listed by Aristotle and Hart, not any dissimilarity, that is most apparent. And the same question arises in each case: why should these be the pleas we recognize? Why is 'I did it in ignorance' an excuse, while 'I did it in malice' is not? Neither Aristotle nor Hart (in the article in question) gives any general principle to justify the particular selection of pleas. But it is surely not an accident that these two philosophers should so often cite the same factors as excusing conditions, nor that so many other people would agree with them. We shall consider the excuses relevant to moral responsibility in this chapter and the next, leaving the rationale of excuses relevant to legal responsibility and punishment until later.

When we hold someone morally responsible for his action, we consider it reasonable to blame him for it if it was a bad action, or to praise him for it if it was a good one. When someone has done something we normally consider bad, we do not hold him morally responsible when we consider it reasonable not to blame him, in virtue of an excuse he has. But it is important that the blame here is moral blame. We can blame the drought for the poor crop, merely assigning a cause to something that we regret, without taking up any moral attitudes at all. But where I blame someone morally for some state of affairs, I am not only regretting the state of affairs and regarding his act or omission as the cause of it, but I am also blaming him for his act or omission. This blaming a person for his act or omission consists in adopting an attitude of disapproval towards him on account of what he has done or failed to do. This attitude may manifest itself in sharp words, in hostile tones of voice or facial expressions, or in other conventional gestures of disapproval. But I may only privately adopt such an attitude, and behave in a perfectly amiable way towards the person I blame.[1] The list of excuses I accept as eliminating blame states those factors which I recognize as making unreasonable any disapproving attitudes towards someone on account of his action.

Anthropologists tell us that in different societies there are very different views as to what factors make it unreasonable to blame someone for something. And in our own society different views are held by different people, and views have changed from one historical period to another, as the history of attitudes towards the mentally ill shows. But the diversity of beliefs occurs inside a context of broad general agreement that one is only justified in blaming someone where he could help doing what he did. And this is no doubt linked to the belief often expressed in the slogan 'ought implies can': the belief that it is only appropriate to say that someone ought to act in a certain way where he can in fact do so. The variety of views as to whom it is reasonable to blame, that are compatible with this generally accepted belief, can largely be explained by the fact that the expression 'I could not help it' can be used to make a number of different claims. I may be trying to excuse myself from blame by making any one of at least three different kinds of claim. I may be claiming that what I did was not an act of mine at all; or I may be claiming that it was an unintentional act; or that it comes under some recognized category of excusable intentional acts. It is worth looking at these claims in more detail.[2]

A. NO ACT

Here I may be claiming that what I did consisted of mere involuntary movements, and did not constitute an action, or else that

---

1 That blaming is not in itself 'doing' something, like scowling, is well brought out in Professor Brandt's paper, 'Blameworthiness and Obligation', in Melden, *Essays in Moral Philosophy*, 1958.
2 The plea of 'no act' is the most powerful of the three to be considered, Dr Eric D'Arcy has said that 'a circumstance such as the physical incapacity to control one's actions is not a mere afterthought which leads us to add a brief rider to our verdict on the act which it concerns: it bears on one of the conditions which must be present in the agent if his act is to be susceptible of moral evaluation at all'. Cf. his *Human Acts*, 1963, p. 87.

my failing to do something was the result of an involuntary lack of movement, and did not constitute an 'act of omission'. In either of these cases, the involuntariness may have resulted from factors internal or external to me. These can be distinguished as cases where I had inadequate capacity and cases where I had inadequate opportunity. There is also a distinction between those involuntary movements over which I have no direct control, such as the onset of a heart attack, and other involuntary movements such as blinking, which occur independently of my decision, but which I can alter directly if I choose.

I can influence indirectly whether or not I have a heart attack, perhaps by eating less or by taking exercise, but I cannot influence it directly as I can the position of my hands. When I blink, this is not normally the result of a decision to do so, but if I wish I may directly influence my blinking. There are, of course, many movements that we do not specifically decide on, and which are yet not involuntary. I do not decide upon any particular movements of my legs when I walk down the street. But there is a way in which one's blinking is more strongly independent of one's decisions than are the movements one makes in walking down the street.

It has been suggested by Professor Hart[1] that the difference between such cases as these last two could be characterized by saying that in the second case, but not in the first, the movements form part of an action which the agent believes himself to be doing, or (in a revised view) that involuntary movements occur 'though the agent had no reason for moving his body in that way'. The first account is open, as Hart admits, to objections concerning the obscurity of the expression 'not forming part of an action', and perhaps also to objections to the expression 'an action which the agent believed himself to be doing', which some might take to include falling downstairs when fully conscious. But the revised account is also open to objection, in that no independent account is provided of what it is to have a reason for moving one's body. Hart allows that the agent had a reason for moving his body where he did it 'just because he wanted to do so'. But the notion of a bodily movement without the person in question having a reason for it seems to need as much elucidation as that of an involuntary movement.

1 *Punishment and Responsibility*, 1968, Ch. 4 and notes.

I am not sure what the best account of involuntary movement would be, but the concept of an 'effort of will' is helpful in its elucidation. For it seems that what distinguishes my blinking from the movement of my legs when I walk down the street is that I can slow down substantially the former only by an effort of will, while I can control the latter with the greatest of ease. The two kinds of involuntary movement, represented by a heart attack and by blinking, are seen as having in common that neither can be directly controlled *without* a special effort, while the first kind cannot even be controlled with one. It is important to recognize here that there is no sharp boundary between these two kinds of involuntary movement. I can, by making a special effort, hold my breath for a matter of minutes. I cannot, even with tremendous effort, hold it for a quarter of an hour. But there is not some precise point (say, three minutes and seven seconds) that marks the difference between what is extremely hard for me to do and what is impossible.

It is worth setting out schematically the kinds of cases where it is correct to plead that no act was performed.

I Involuntary Movements

a *Capacity*
  (i) Outside my direct control: e.g. a heart attack.
  (ii) Can only directly be controlled by a great effort of will: e.g. a reflex eye blink.

b *Opportunity*
  (i) Outside my direct control: e.g. my hand is forced by someone much stronger than me.
  (ii) Can only directly be controlled by a great effort of will: e.g. my hand is forced by someone a bit stronger than me.

II Involuntary Lack of Movement (No 'act of omission')

a *Capacity*
  (i) Outside my direct control: e.g. where I am paralysed.
  (ii) Can only directly be controlled by a great effort of will: e.g. where I am in a state of extreme exhaustion.

b *Opportunity*

  (i) Outside my direct control: e.g. I am tied up with un-
      breakable wire rope.
  (ii) Can only directly be controlled by a great effort of will:
      e.g. I am held down by someone a bit stronger than me.

It is important that, in each of the four general categories, the
distinction between (i) and (ii) is one that corresponds to no
sharply detectable borderline in nature. In the case of a man in
a state of extreme exhaustion, one cannot point to the moment
at which movements that were possible with enormous effort
become impossible. And it is clear that there is no sharp boundary
between an ordinary effort of will and a 'great' one. But the need
for a slight effort of will to make myself get out of bed in the
morning does not make my staying in bed involuntary, nor does
it excuse my act of omission in not keeping a breakfast
appointment.

B. UNINTENTIONAL ACTS

When I say 'I couldn't help it', I may not be denying that 'it' was
an act of mine, but rather claiming that it was an unintentional
act. Here again, it may have been an action I performed, or it
may have been an act of omission. In the case of an action I performed, it will count as unintentional if I did it by accident, by
mistake or inadvertently. It is not clear that these three types of
case are the only ones. If I did it in my sleep, under hypnosis, or
when drugged, should I plead mistake, or was it inadvertence?
Or should such cases form a separate category? (Or three separate
categories?)

  Leaving aside these special problems, unintentional acts of
omission seem to fall into the same classes of accident, mistake
and inadvertence. It was an accidental omission if I set off to go
and do it, but on the way the car broke down. If I went to the
wrong place, it was a mistake rather than an accident. And, if I
forgot altogether, this was inadvertence.

  Accident, mistake or inadvertence are always enough to establish that the act or omission was unintentional, but the fact that
it was unintentional only counts as an excuse where negligence

was not involved. If the matter was so important that I should have made sure the car did not break down or else should have used some other means of transport, then I was negligent. It is always possible to disagree about what counts as negligence, since opinions may vary as to how much care and attention are due. But the fact that I did something (or failed to do it) unintentionally only justifies the claim that 'I could not help it' where I was not negligent.

C. EXCUSABLE INTENTIONAL ACTS

For the moment, the only class of excusable intentional acts I shall mention is that where a plea of excusing circumstances would be appropriate. I can only plead excusing circumstances where the situation was such that it would be unreasonable to expect me to do otherwise than I did. Three main types of case come to mind:

a *Threats:* These can be against me or against other people.

b *Torture:* I might give way either under torture myself, or else do so when someone else is tortured until I give way.

c *Extreme need:* e.g. extreme hunger, thirst or pain may make me steal food, water or drugs. The need in question may be my own or may be that of another person or other people.

As in other cases, these acts in excusing circumstances can be actions that I perform or else acts of omission. And these acts are especially contentious examples of where 'I could not help it', as it is so very open to dispute how much my doing what I should must be to my disadvantage before it becomes unreasonable to require me to do it. In deciding which excuses of this kind to accept for a particular 'offence', there is a whole range of possible attitudes of varying toughness or leniency. And circumstances not held to excuse the action can be held to mitigate it.

4

DETERMINISM AND BLAME

How intoxicating to feel like God the Father and to hand
out definitive testimonials of bad character and habits.

Camus

We adopt attitudes of disapproval towards people on account
of what they do, or what they fail to do, and we feel that these
attitudes are only justified where the person blamed could help
his act or omission. According to an argument mentioned at the
start of the previous chapter, the truth of determinism would
entail that I could never act differently from how I do act, and so
would presumably never be able to help what I did. Where my
act could have been predicted on the basis of a set of true causal
laws, together with statements of the relevant initial conditions,
I could not have acted otherwise. For, to have done so would
have been to falsify at least one of a set of statements which,
ex hypothesi, are all true.

William James made a famous distinction between 'soft' and
'hard' determinism.[1] A soft determinist is someone who thinks
determinism is true, but that this does not undermine any of our
normal moral attitudes towards people. Schlick's views are typical
here. Hard determinists are those who think determinism true,
but who reject any attempts to reconcile this with our present
moral attitudes. In this chapter, it will be argued that, while soft

1 In an otherwise unmemorable essay: 'The Dilemma of Determinism',
The Unitarian Review, 1884, reprinted in James (ed. Castell), *Essays in Prag-
matism,* 1948.

determinism as previously expounded is incomplete, we are not forced to accept hard determinism. The argument for hard determinism mentioned above rests on the assumption that sentences like 'I could not help it' or 'I could not have done otherwise' are used to make only a single kind of claim. But we have seen, in the previous chapter, that at least three different kinds of claim may be made. It may be claimed that the event in question was not an act at all, or that it was an unintentional act not involving negligence, or that it was an excusable intentional act. The argument here against hard determinism will be that it is up to us to choose which excuses to accept, and that, even if we decide to absolve people from blame where they cannot do otherwise than what they do, we need not accept that determinism entails that they 'cannot do otherwise' *in the relevant sense*. But, in order to argue this, it is necessary to show that we are in a position to decide what factors we will accept as excuses absolving a person from blame.

Is blame the sort of thing that can be dispensed or withheld according to criteria of our own choosing? Or is it logically impossible to hold certain factual beliefs about a person's action without blaming him? Or, on the other hand, could we not altogether give up blaming people for what they do? It is some-times suggested, particularly by hard determinists, that the only civilized or rationally defensible course for us would be to stop blaming people in any circumstances.

1   A WORLD WITHOUT BLAME

There seems no logical impossibility about a world in which we never disapproved of any person, although we retained our prefer-ences for some courses of action over others. We could exhort people not to do the actions we object to, and to do those we preferred. After the performance of an action, we could express pleasure or displeasure, as we do when, on a cold morning, a car either starts or fails to start. But, just as we regret the failure to start without disapproving of the car itself, so we could dislike actions but not disapprove of people.

In such a world, 'blaming' someone for something would be like blaming the bad weather for the disappointing holiday. In our present scheme of blame, we insist on blaming people only for what they can help, just because to blame a person for an action is more than merely to say that he has brought about something we object to. We disapprove, not merely of the action or its consequences, but of him. Involved in our present practice of blame is a kind of moral accounting, where a person's actions are recorded in an informal balance sheet, with the object of assessing his moral worth.[1] And with praise, we distinguish between praising something wholly or largely beyond a person's control, as when we praise someone's beauty or intelligence, and that praise on the other hand that is relevant to the moral balance sheet. At present, we may criticize someone's stupidity, but, thinking it largely outside his control, we may not regard this as relevant to the assessment of his moral worth. In a world without this kind of moral accounting, all praise and dispraise of people would in this respect become like praise of someone's beauty or criticism of their ugliness.

It is sometimes suggested that such a world would be a cold world, in which the spontaneity and warmth of our present relationships with each other would be replaced by the kind of calculating manipulation that now characterizes our relations with machines. But to dispense with moral accounting would not be to dispense with friendship and hostility. At present, many of our likes and dislikes are based on characteristics largely outside people's control, and our recognition that this is so does not diminish the strength of our attitudes. And to refrain from moral condemnation of people need not involve seeing them merely as objects to be manipulated for our own ends: we can still take their interests into account, and we can still love or hate them as we do now.

It may be objected that if, in a world without blame, we were able to disapprove of people's actions and characteristics (which are often identifiable through actions), this would not be significantly different from a world like our own. For, it may be said, to disapprove of people just is to disapprove of their actions and characteristics. But this objection misses a vital feature of the disapproval of people that constitutes blame. For purposes of blame, we identify a person with some of his characteristics rather than others. In the explanation of an action, or of the failure

1   Cf. Feinberg, *Action and Responsibility, loc. cit.*

64

of an action, the concepts on the one hand of 'will', 'want', 'desire' and 'try', interlock with the concepts of 'power', 'capacity', 'ability' and 'opportunity' on the other. Professor Hampshire has made the point in this way:

> The fact that a man failed in his attempt to climb the mountain is not by itself sufficient to establish that he could not do so. One needs the assumption that he still wanted to, and, consequently, that he was trying to, and that his failure was not attributable to lack of will. Granted this assumption, and only granted this, and given that the normal background conditions presupposed are not suddenly changed, it does indeed follow from the fact that the performance was in fact a failure that the power was at that moment lacking.[1]

When someone fails, this is because he lacks the will or the power. When he lacks the power, we see this for moral purposes as something 'external' in some way to the person himself. When he lacks the will, we are normally prepared to blame him, because we see lack of will as something 'internal' to the person himself.

The metaphorical distinction between what is internal and what is external to a person arises in the context of a morality of intention. The contrast between a moral concern with intention and a moral concern with consequences is familiar in ethics. It was brought out clearly by Mill, when he said that 'utilitarian moralists have gone beyond almost all others in affirming that the motive has nothing to do with the morality of the action, though much with the worth of the agent'.[2] Mill, as a utilitarian, judged the moral worth of actions solely on the basis of their consequences. Some utilitarians are concerned with motives and intentions only to the extent that they influence the outcome of acts. But, opposed to such views are various moralities of intention or motive. These include Kantian moralities and some varieties of Christian morality, the latter preserving something of the spirit of the obscure remark that 'whosoever looketh on a woman to lust after her hath committed adultery with her already in his heart'.[3] On these views, an act is morally good if well-intentioned, even if its consequences turn out to be disastrous.

1 *Freedom of the Individual,* 1965, Ch. 1.
2 *Utilitarianism,* Ch. 2.   3   Matthew, 5.

And equally, an ill-intentioned act is a bad act, even if it turns out to have the most desirable consequences. It may be that these two kinds of morality can more nearly be reconciled than is sometimes thought. Perhaps intentions are only good when directed towards good consequences. But a pure morality of intention is concerned with the moral worth of a person, rather than with the outcome of his acts. And it is this concern that makes blaming people differ from merely disapproving of what they do.

I shall in this context use the word 'intention' in such a way as to make it a necessary truth that, where someone fails to do something that he attempts, to the extent that this cannot be explained in terms of his limited abilities or opportunities, it can be explained in terms of the weakness of his intention. It is also a necessary truth that, to the extent that his failure cannot be explained in terms of his weak intention, it can be explained in terms of his limited abilities or opportunities. (These remarks should not be construed as making determinism true by definition.) This use of 'intention' corresponds to the use of 'will' in 'weakness of will'. Those who believe in blaming people believe in disapproving of people as well as in disapproving of actions. And, for purposes of blame, we see the real nature of the person by examining his intentions rather than his abilities or his opportunities. Blame as we know it involves identifying the person who is the object of blame with his intentions, and treating other factors influencing his conduct as external. Even his mental abilities are seen as being possessed by the person rather than as being part of the person blamed.

But not all intentions are seen as internal to the person blamed. Sometimes a person's intention is one that he does not identify with, or endorse, and is one that he would prefer to be without. A drug addict's intention to pursue his addiction may often be of this kind. Then it appears that he is not capable of altering his intention, and this lack of capacity may well exempt him from blame. To sum up crudely: for purposes of blame, a person is his intentions, except where his intentions are unalterable as the addict's are.

We could (logically) abandon all moralities of intention, with a resulting abandonment of our practice of weighing up the moral worth of people. If we did this, the type of blame under discussion here would vanish. Talking of the 'reactive' attitudes, that include blame, Professor Strawson has said that 'in the absence of *any* forms of these attitudes, it is doubtful whether we should have anything that *we* could find intelligible as a system of human relationships, as human society'.[1] Even if this doubt is well founded, it is insufficient to establish that the retention of blame is either necessary or desirable. We might retain all our other reactive attitudes but this one, without dehumanizing our relationships with each other. And, even if blame were in some way essential for the maintenance of the other reactive attitudes, Strawson's claim does not entail the impossibility (empirical or logical) of our abandoning them all. And the undesirability of such a step needs to be established by a stronger argument than the assertion that the resulting state of affairs would not seem *to us* to be an intelligible human society.

But, if it is possible for us to abandon our practice of blaming people, and not clearly undesirable, it is not clearly desirable either. It may be that, when people refrain from behaving badly, they do so partly because they dislike being blamed. Perhaps the knowledge that other people make moral judgments about oneself has a deterrent effect that would not be adequately replaced by the knowledge that they made moral judgments about actions. We do often strongly dislike being blamed, even when the blame is not deliberately expressed. It may be said that, in a world in which we never actually blamed people, we could have the same beneficial effect on conduct by expressing a disapproval of people that we did not actually feel. But this is open to objections on grounds of honesty. Such deception would also very likely be ineffective. If we all took part in the pretence, we should probably see through it in each other. And even if only some of us set up as moral judges, it is not clear that we should succeed, either in influencing the conduct of others or in sustaining the pretence.

It may be that our willingness to make moral judgments about people is not the most attractive aspect of our relationships as they are now. But, even if a world without blame might be less

1 'Freedom and Resentment', *Proceedings of the British Academy*, 1962, p. 210. For criticism of Strawson's views, cf. Downie, *Objective and Reactive Attitudes,* and Llewelyn, *The Inconceivability of Pessimistic Determinism,* both in *Analysis,* 1966.

strange or hateful than is sometimes suggested, it is very hard at present to calculate with any confidence the social gains and losses it would involve. And, even if such a world is logically possible, it is hard to see it coming easily. Attitudes of disapproval of people on account of their actions are deeply ingrained in our present social life, as Strawson has emphasized.[1] It is not clear what psychological changes would have to come about in us for these attitudes to be renounced. For these reasons, while I do not wish to assert dogmatically that a world without blame would be impossible or undesirable, I shall assume for the rest of this book that for the moment we will continue to make moral judgments about people.

But, within the framework of our judgments of people, there recur the questions asked earlier. Why do we accept the excuses that we do? What do the pleas of 'no act' or of 'unintentional act' have in common with each other, or with those intentional acts that are held to be excusable? The answers to these questions often take the form either of saying that in these cases attitudes of disapproval would be pointless, or else that they would be unjust.

2 WHEN BLAME IS SAID TO BE POINTLESS

As we have seen, expressions of blame often function like informal punishments, being used to modify a person's conduct. When parents express disapproval of what their children do, they often have this modification of conduct as a conscious goal. The means by which expressions of blame alter behaviour vary. The child may behave differently because he sees the validity of his parents' reasons for disapproval, or else merely because he dislikes being the object of disapproval. Sometimes, when blame is expressed there is no conscious attempt to alter behaviour: after a minor car crash, expressions of disapproval may serve as an emotional release in the same way as swear-words do. But, whatever the motives underlying expressions of blame, it is unpleasant to be on the receiving end of them.[2] Because of this,

1 'Freedom and Resentment', *Proceedings of the British Academy*, 1962, p. 210.
2 This is why we are more concerned with excuses than with modest disclaimers: it is more important to avoid unfair or pointless blame than to restrict praise to appropriate occasions, which would just be ungenerous.

blame may work, as punishments are said to do, to make the person blamed mend his ways, or else to deter other people from following his example. The point of blame, it may be said, is its effectiveness in these ways.

In criticism of this view, it is sometimes said that so functional an account of blame distorts our view of it by over-emphasizing its results. Strawson has said,

> It is far from wrong to emphasize the efficacy of all those practices which express or manifest our moral attitudes, in regulating behaviour in ways considered desirable; or to add that when certain of our beliefs about the efficacy of some of these practices turn out to be false, then we may have good reason for dropping or modifying those practices. What *is* wrong is to forget that these practices, and their reception, the reactions to them, really *are* expressions of our moral attitudes and not merely devices we calculatingly employ for regulative purposes. Our practices do not merely exploit our natures, they express them. Indeed the very understanding of the kind of efficacy these expressions of our attitudes have turns on our remembering this.[1]

But, accepting Strawson's point that expressions of blame are not merely regulative devices, one might still hold that, in view of the discomfort they cause, they should be justified by reference to the purpose they serve.

It is suggested that expressions of blame for something done are pointless where the event in question did not constitute an action, or else where it was an unintentional action. This is essentially the same as Schlick's argument about the pointlessness of punishment in such cases. It is said that blame is useless as a means of altering the behaviour of the person whose involuntary movement or unintentional act it was. If we want to stop someone shooting animals, we may deter him from doing so by showing him that, every time he acts on a decision to shoot one, he will be blamed. When he is deciding whether or not to shoot another animal, the fact that past cases of unintentional shooting have not led to blame will be irrelevant to his decision, so long as he knows that all cases of deliberate shooting do result in blame.

There are objections to this argument. One is that blaming a

1 *loc. cit.*

69

man for unintentional acts may be useful, in that this may cause him to take more trouble to avoid accidents, mistakes or inadvertence next time. Another is that men do not always decide rationally, so that previous blame for what was unintentional may strengthen someone's resolve not to do that kind of thing intentionally. And there is the objection, made in criticism of Schlick's views on punishment, that to blame people whenever they did something of a certain kind, whether intentionally or not, might more powerfully deter other people than would blame for intentional acts only. So it is not clear that to blame someone for anything other than an intentional act is always pointless. There may be a reasonable presumption that blame is likely to be less effective in such cases, but that it is quite pointless is an empirical claim which, although sometimes made, has never been adequately supported.

Is it pointless to blame someone for an intentional act done in what are normally thought to be excusing circumstances? Where the agent acted in circumstances such that we think it unreasonable to expect him to act differently, we usually do not blame him. But surely expressions of blame are not in all such cases pointless? If a man betrays a secret under torture, it is perhaps unreasonable to say that he ought not to do so. It may be pointless to blame him since the torture may be so severe that the desire to avoid blame will carry no weight. But, in other cases, desire not to be blamed might be a stronger motive than the incentive to do the wrong act, and might make all the difference to the outcome of the decision. It might be that fewer people would be prepared to give way to coercion or blackmail if attitudes of even greater disapproval were adopted and expressed in such cases. Again, there may be a reasonable presumption that blame is likely to be less effective in many such cases, but one cannot know without evidence that it would always be pointless.

3 WHEN BLAME IS SAID TO BE UNJUST

It is often said to be unjust to blame someone for what he could not help doing. It is possible on this basis to defend the recognition of all the pleas so far mentioned, since they can all be held to support the claim, 'I could not help it.' To call something 'unjust' is *prima facie* to criticize it adversely. Politicians against injustice are as numerous as preachers opposed to sin. We expect people to be in favour of what they consider just, unless they say that in a particular case other considerations must over-ride the claims of justice. But to call something 'just' is less empty of descriptive content than to call it 'right'. I may think it right that medical research or art galleries should be subsidized by the government, but I am unlikely to say that this would be 'just'. There are broad factual criteria for the use of this word, which set limits to what I can approve of in this way.[1]

Philosophical discussions of justice commonly distinguish between 'distributive' and 'retributive' justice, and, although it can be argued that this distinction is not entirely happy, it makes a convenient starting point. In considering distributive justice, one finds broad agreement about the most general principles, combined with great disagreement as to which courses of action are just.[2] Many would accept some such general formula of distributive justice as 'in the distribution of benefits or burdens, people should be treated equally except where there is some relevant difference between them'. This is not a completely empty principle, for a commitment to it places the burden of argument on those who treat men unequally. But it will not settle the most interesting disputes about distributive justice, since these concern the question of which differences are relevant. When people argue about the just distribution of a society's wealth among its members, disputes centre on the relevance of differences. To some, no appeal to special circumstances can alter the basic injustice of paying one man more than another. To others, it will seem obviously unjust to pay people equally when some have greater needs. To yet others, it will seem unjust to pay the person who works harder no more than the person who works less.

Through the history of philosophical discussion of justice, there has run the ambiguity noticed by Aristotle, when he distinguishes between the sense in which justice 'is not part of virtue but virtue entire' on the one hand and 'the justice which is a part of virtue' on the other.[3] Some people talk of justice in such a way that the just course of action is by definition that which, all

1 Cf. Hart, *The Concept of Law,* 1961, Ch. 8.
2 Cf. Perelman, *The Idea of Justice and the Problems of Argument,* 1963, Ch. I.
3 *Nicomachean Ethics,* Book 5.

things considered, one morally ought to take. Injustice and wrong
are thus equivalent. But it is arguably more useful to accept the
limiting criteria mentioned above, thus treating justice as only
one virtue among many. Then, in deciding what one ought to
do it will be necessary to weigh the claims of justice against such
possibly competing claims as those of freedom or the maximizing
of happiness.[1] One could thus hold that, if a just distribution of
income led to more than a certain degree of economic inefficiency,
this might be too high a price for it.

There is a case for linking distributive justice to the notion of
desert, and hence with 'retributive justice'. This would involve
only recognizing those things about him that a man can help, as
being relevant to the justice of treating him differently from
others when distributing benefits or burdens. Thus, differential
rewards for making greater or smaller contributions to the community by one's work, would only be just to the extent that the
size of one's contribution was within one's control. Great
strength or high intelligence may increase the usefulness of one's
work, but it is only just to reward them to the extent that they
are not the result of innate factors, or of other factors beyond
one's control. Those born with physical incapacities or mental
deficiencies cannot justly be rewarded less than others for their
contribution to society. It may be that there is a case for income
differentials based on needs or talents that are largely outside our
control, but it is possible[2] to see this as a case for allowing justice
to be over-ridden by other considerations. To suppose that any
differences whatever between people can be relevant to the justice
of unequal distribution between them, is only to prolong the confusion between justice as 'virtue entire' and as 'a part of virtue'.

'Retributive' justice is too narrowly named for what it encom-
passes. It tends, as a result, to be restricted to the context of
punishment, in isolation from other questions about what people
deserve. Retributive justice concerns giving people what they
deserve, but they deserve praise or reward, as well as blame or
punishment. There are various possible principles based on
desert. There is the 'positive' principle that people should always
get what they deserve, and distinct from this is the 'negative'

1 Cf. Barry, *Political Argument,* 1965, Ch. 1, for a discussion of 'trade-off'
relations between different values.
2 Though perhaps less plausible in the case of needs.

principle that people should never get what they do not deserve. What one deserves may be good or bad: a Nobel Prize or a prison sentence. One might for all cases hold the positive principle, or the negative one, or both. Another possibility is the bleak combination of the negative principle for the distribution of good things and the positive principle for the distribution of bad things. Or there is the more generous combination of the negative principle for the distribution of bad things and the positive principle for good things.

Since it is disagreeable to be disapproved of, the view that it is unjust to blame someone for what he could not help results from the negative principle of desert applied to the distribution of bad things. But what is it to 'deserve' something? One comes to deserve something good or bad by behaving better or worse than one could have done. And here reference to what one could have done is reference to one's capacities or one's opportunities. The soldier deserves a medal because he was brave where he had the opportunity to be cowardly. The criminal deserves to be punished, we suppose, until we discover that he was mentally ill in such a way that he lacked the capacity to conform to the law. The notion of desert functions within a morality of intention and, as we have seen, 'intention' within such a morality is contrasted with capacities and opportunities.

Our recognition of all the excuses so far listed can be defended by an appeal to justice. We think it unfair to adopt an attitude of disapproval towards someone on account of an act or omission, where this was something outside his control. What is within my control depends on my capacities and opportunities. We have seen that all cases of involuntary movement and of involuntary lack of movement can be classified either as cases of impaired capacity or as cases of lack of opportunity. And where what I did was an action, but an unintentional one, I can reasonably claim that, because I did not realize what I was doing, I did not have the opportunity to correct my conduct. (To say that I should have realized what I was doing, and hence that I was negligent, is among other things to say that I had a reasonable opportunity to avoid getting into such a state of ignorance.) And cases where I act intentionally, but under pressure of threats, torture or extreme need, can be seen as cases where my opportunities are circumscribed.

73

4 CAUSATION AND RESPONSIBILITY

The argument for the view that an agent should not be held responsible for his acts if they are causally determined cannot rest on the pointlessness of blame in such cases. We have seen that blame is not clearly ineffective even in cases where there are other excuses that we recognize. But it seems merely absurd to suppose that wherever there is a causal explanation for my conduct, I will be impervious to the influence of the disapproving attitudes of others. Combining this view with determinism would generate the false consequence that no one ever alters his conduct as the result of being blamed.

The view that determinism makes all blame unfair has greater apparent plausibility. We have seen that this view depends upon the claim that, where a prediction of what I will do is entailed by a set of true statements about causal laws and initial conditions, it is not possible that I will do anything else. It is suggested that this makes it true that I cannot help what I do, and that it is therefore unjust to blame me.

But this argument rests on a confusion between two kinds of claim.[1] There are claims about what is possible for me in terms of my capacities and opportunities; and claims about what is possible (logically) given the truth of certain statements. We have seen that what is just is linked to capacities and opportunities. What people deserve is dependent in part on their capacities and on the opportunities open to them. To show that the truth of determinism makes all blame unjust, one would either have to adopt new standards of justice or else show that determinism entails that no one ever has both the capacity and the opportunity to act differently from how he does act. It is a consequence of determinism that all courses of action except one are ruled out as being incompatible with a set of true statements. But this is not peculiar to the predictions of the determinist. True statements about the past have the same consequences. It is true that yesterday I stayed indoors instead of going out. So I cannot (logically) have spent yesterday out of doors, for if I had done so this would falsify the statement which we know to be true: that

1 Discussed in (e.g.) Hampshire, *Freedom of the Individual*, 1965, and Ayers, *The Refutation of Determinism*, 1968, Chs. 2 and 3.

I stayed indoors. But this does not mean that I lacked either the capacity or the opportunity to go out. Similarly, on the basis of causal laws, it may in principle be predictable that I will go out rather than stay in tomorrow. But this in no way shows that tomorrow I will lack either the capacity or the opportunity to stay indoors.

Those who think that mere causal explanation of an action eliminates the agent's responsibility for it have three courses open to them. They can say that, in the light of determinism, we should modify our concepts of capacity and opportunity. They can reject the view that what we deserve varies according to our capacities and opportunities. Or they can give up the notion of desert altogether. But each of these alternatives presents difficulties. To 'modify' the concepts of capacity and opportunity, in such a way that it becomes true that we never have the capacity and opportunity to do anything different from what we in fact do, would be to distort those words beyond recognition. And the other two alternatives involve more radical changes of attitude than one may wish to accept.

If we were to sever the links between what people deserve and their capacities and opportunities, we might make the blameworthiness of an agent for his action depend on the absence of a causal explanation for what he does. Then, either we could take the view that no one is ever justly blamed, or we could simply hope that scientists never succeed in proving determinism true.

Taking the first view comes in practice to the same as altogether giving up the notion of blame being linked to desert. It is not clear whether or not it would be psychologically possible for us to give up disapproving of people on account of what they do. But, even if it is not possible to give up blaming people, it seems possible to accept that one's attitudes of disapproval are not justifiable, as a man who feels hostile to homosexuals may recognize that his attitude is not rational and, since people are rarely homosexual from choice, unfair. Yet if one thinks all blame equally undeserved, it is impossible to make a special case for the unfairness of blaming those who lacked the capacity or opportunity to conform to whatever moral standards are in question. The man who has a heart attack when driving, and so runs over pedestrians, would be no less liable to blame than the driver who deliberately runs over someone he does not like.

At present most of us do not take this view: we think it right to single out those who cannot help what they do, and to absolve them from the blame that attaches to those who deliberately do wrong in circumstances where they were able not to. It is not clear that anything would be gained by abandoning this distinction.

An alternative to our present practice of making desert depend on capacity and opportunity is to make the blameworthiness of actions depend on their not being caused. If we take this view, and yet reject the view that no blame is ever justified, we are left simply having to hope that determinism is never proved true. This position is reminiscent of that of some theists, who have argued that we need to postulate the existence of God to explain certain facts for which we have no adequate scientific explanation. The origins of the universe, of life, or of consciousness, have all at various times been held to be explicable only in terms of divine intervention. But attempts to show that we do have need of this hypothesis are embarrassed by the development of purely empirical explanations of the same facts. As long as science advances, this kind of God will be increasingly redundant. If we see human responsibility in this way, we will be placed in the unhappy position of cherishing obscurantist hopes for the defeat of the scientific enterprise. And even those untroubled by this might wonder if they want the range of actions for which we are responsible to correspond so exactly to the range of our ignorance.

The suggestion here is that it is often useful to hold people liable to blame when their action has a causal explanation, and that the proposal that we should regard such blame as unfair has little to commend it. Where I have the opportunity to act differently from how I do act, the unfairness of blaming me for choosing badly is linked to my lack of capacity rather than to *any* causal explanation. But it may be objected that questions of capacity cannot be so clearly separated from questions of causation.

Surely, it may be said, determinism must entail that, in any situation as it is, I do not have the capacity to take any course of action except the one predictable on the basis of the causal laws? That I stayed indoors yesterday does not show that I lack in general the capacity to leave the house: I am neither paralysed nor a prisoner. But does determinism not perhaps show that, with circumstances as they were yesterday, I lacked the capacity to leave the house on that particular day?

One way of attempting to defeat this suggestion is to make the claim, for which I surely have good grounds, that if I had chosen to go out I would have succeeded in going out. It has been persuasively argued that such a statement is not equivalent to the claim that I had the capacity to go out.[1] The capacity to leave the house falls into two parts: the capacity to take the decision to do this and the capacity to put one's decision into effect. Whatever the limitations of the claim that, if I had chosen to go out, I would have succeeded, its truth does at least demonstrate the existence of the second capacity: to put this decision into effect.

So, given that, if I had chosen to act differently, I would have succeeded in so acting, the claim that determinism abolishes our capacities to act differently from how we do act can be narrowed down. This can only have plausibility when it is suggested that what determinism shows us to lack is the capacity to take decisions that we do not take. It may be said that, while yesterday I was capable of executing any decision to go out, I was not then capable of taking such a decision.

But the argument even for this refined view seems to rest on the same confusion as before. I see no reason to deny that the expression 'he could not have decided otherwise' can be used to express a claim which determinism would prove to be true for

1 Cf. J. L. Austin, 'Ifs and Cans', *Proceedings of the Aristotelian Society*, 1956–7, reprinted in *Philosophical Papers*, 1961.
Austin's arguments there do not seem to me to tell against the view, to be urged later in this book, that the crucial test for whether someone could have done something is whether he would have done it, given a strong enough motive for doing so. Actions seem to me to result from the combination of a preponderant motive with what is described by what Austin calls the 'all-in' sense of 'can'. I take it that someone can do something in the 'all-in' sense when he has the opportunity to do it, and the ability both to decide to do it and to put his decision into effect. A golfer who missed a putt when he has a preponderant motive not to do so, must *at that moment* have lacked ability to hole it in those circumstances. Where unfavourable circumstances play a crucial role, we lay the blame on his lack of opportunity to exercise the ability he displays in better circumstances. But where the circumstances were good and the golfer has a preponderant motive for succeeding, we can only explain his failure by supposing that the ability he normally has must have deserted him at that moment. Unless we accept that abilities can sometimes fluctuate, such a failure must remain entirely mysterious. Cf. Nowell Smith's reply to Austin, 'Ifs and Cans', *Theoria*, 1960.

any decision. Given the truth of certain statements of causal laws and initial conditions, the outcome of the decision could not (logically) be otherwise. But, this does not show that I lacked the capacity to decide otherwise. I may decide to have a drink in a pub, and so may an alcoholic. The fact that a statement that this will be my decision is entailed by certain other statements does not seem sufficient to show that I am no more capable of the opposite decision than is the alcoholic. The capacity to decide is in this respect no different from the capacity to do anything else: an athlete is at this moment capable of doing things I cannot do, even if at present he is relaxing instead, and I am capable of deciding against a drink even when I am just deciding in favour of one.

5 CONCLUSIONS

a. Rejection of Hard Determinism

The view that determinism, if true, must undermine our beliefs about moral responsibility has been stated by Professor Berlin. Speaking of 'social determinism', he says,

> And it may indeed, be a true doctrine. But if it is true, and if we begin to take it seriously, then, indeed, the changes in the whole of our language, our moral terminology, our attitudes toward one another, our views of history, of society, and of everything else will be too profound to be even adumbrated. The concepts of praise and blame, inno-cence and guilt and individual responsibility from which we started are but a small element in the structure, which would collapse or disappear. . . . Our words – our modes of speech and thought – would be transformed in literally unimaginable ways; the notions of choice, of responsibility, of freedom, are so deeply embedded in our outlook that our new life, as creatures in a world genuinely lacking in these concepts, can, I should maintain, be conceived by us only with the greatest difficulty.[1]

1 Berlin, 'Historical Inevitability', *Auguste Comte Memorial Trust Lecture*, 1953, reprinted in Berlin, *Four Essays on Liberty*, 1969. This quotation is from p. 113 of the latter book. Berlin himself cannot be called a 'hard determinist', since he is not committed to the truth of any version of determinism.

It is hard to know what to reply to someone who warns us of changes too profound to be even adumbrated. It is not clear why we should accept that these changes are entailed by the truth of determinism in the absence of detailed supporting argument. That determinism must undermine our moral attitudes is often presented as a truth that is intuitively obvious without need of argument. But one can construct a line of reasoning that makes this conclusion plausible. This reasoning goes from 'all human behaviour is governed by causal laws' to 'no one can ever do anything different from what he does' and then to 'blame is always undeserved'.

The argument used here against hard determinism claims that there is an equivocation in 'no one can ever do any different from what he does'. It was suggested in the previous chapter that 'I could not help it' can be used to make a variety of different claims. The same holds for the parallel 'I could not do anything different'. If this sentence is used to make one of the various possible claims about my lack of capacity or opportunity, it is not entailed by determinism. And the sense in which, if determinism is true, 'I could not do anything different' has nothing to do with my capacities or opportunities, and hence nothing to do with whether or not I deserve to be blamed.

But the rejection of hard determinism does not merely turn on the negative point that the most plausible argument in its favour is equivocal. This rejection is also based on the positive claim that to blame someone is a matter of adopting a certain attitude towards him, and that we are free to decide upon the general principles to be used as a basis for absolving people from our disapproval.

To disapprove of people, rather than of their actions alone, involves adopting a certain attitude towards them. Actions are often short-lived. People on the whole persist through a longer stretch of time. Some people only enter our consciousness in connection with some particular action: perhaps we only meet them once, or we only hear of them because they get into the newspapers. Then, if we disapprove of their action, we may also disapprove of them, but our adopting this attitude towards them may be of little significance. But most of us occupy points in a complex network of more persisting relationships. When I disapprove of the action of someone with whom I have a fairly substantial relationship, my attitude towards him on account of this will to some degree modify my continuing estimate of him as a person.

In the context of a morality of intention, these attitudes are responses to the intention or will underlying acts or omissions, rather than to the person's abilities or opportunities. We could, I have argued, envisage a society in which either this distinction between will and ability was not morally important, or else where these moral attitudes towards people were simply not adopted. But our present attitudes do exist in this context of identifying people, for the purposes of moral appraisal, with their intentions. And the notion of 'intention' in this context is contrasted with abilities and opportunities. It is thus correct to assert, as the hard determinist does, that our disapproving attitudes towards a person do presuppose that 'he could have done otherwise'. They presuppose that he had the ability and opportunity to act differently. But the hard determinist must go further than this to establish his case. He must show that determinism entails that no one ever has the opportunity and ability to do otherwise than he does. It is this claim that I have argued is false.

It may appear that the argument used against this hard determinist claim involves an infinite regress. The argument can be briefly stated in terms of a crude classification of the machinery of action. In this classification, acts are the product of desire, opportunity and ability. It is only where a bad act or omission results from a bad desire (or lack of good desire) that one should be blamed. But a bad desire may be one that the agent desires to change, yet is unable to do so. It is only when he does not desire to change his first desire that he should be blamed. But how about his second-order desire? Has he the ability to alter this? One can see the possibility of regress. The situation can be represented diagrammatically (see facing page).

Looked at in this way, it may appear that one would only be entitled to blame someone after an infinitely protracted investigation of his psychology.[1] But, since it is up to us to decide when to disapprove of people, we can make a cut-off point where we choose. We might say that a person is blameworthy where his

[1] There is a similar regress argument, stated in terms of volitions, in Broad, 'Determinism, Indeterminism and Libertarianism', in *Ethics and the History of Philosophy*, 1952.

bad action was one he desired to perform (i.e. where he had the opportunity and ability not to perform it) and where this desire was not one he desired to change (rather than one he was unable to change). We might decide to reject as irrelevant to our attitudes any investigation of his ability or desire to change this second-order desire. It does not greatly matter if someone wishes

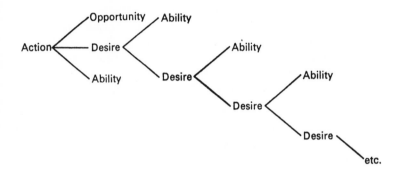

to push the cut-off point a bit further back. It would be a pity to make the cut-off point any less far back, as this would make us unable to excuse the addict who steals drugs because he desires them, but hates having this desire. We do not have to think in terms of a rigid cut-off point: blame is a matter of degree, and we can blame someone more or less according to how far back one has to go before finding a desire that he desires to change but cannot.

The case against hard determinism rests on the variety of uses of 'I could not have done anything different', on only one of which is this true in virtue of determinism. Our moral attitudes towards people depend on their opportunities and abilities. (Although 'how far back' this goes depends on our, perhaps arbitrary, decision.) We would only need to accept hard determinism if it could be shown that determinism makes all talk of having the opportunity and ability to act differently an illusion. This claim has been rejected here.

b.   The Incompleteness of Soft Determinism

The present argument lends some support to the empiricist

philosophers, from Hobbes to Schlick and Ayer, in their soft determinism: their attempts to reconcile determinism with responsibility. But there are reasons for saying that the standard empiricist solution is too hasty. Ayer has expressed some doubts about it.[1] He says

> The main objections to it are that the boundaries of constraint are not at all easy to draw with any precision; and that even if they could be drawn at all precisely, the distinction for which they are needed seems rather arbitrary. Why should a man be praised or blamed if his actions are brought about in one way, and acquitted if they are brought about in another? In either case they are equally the product of his heredity and environment.

Ayer's second objection, that the distinction is arbitrary, seems only a polemical way of making the point accepted here, that any general policy of having or not having restrictions on when to blame people depends on a moral choice. I think it fair to blame someone for a bad act where he had the capacity and opportunity to avoid it, but unfair to blame someone where he did not have the capacity and opportunity to do otherwise. To take a different view is to choose to ignore considerations of justice. It is not clear that a belief in justice is any more arbitrary than any other moral belief.[2]

Ayer's other point is that the boundaries of constraint are not easy to draw with any precision. Here we can distinguish between different types of impairment of capacity or opportunity that might come under the heading of 'constraint'. We have looked at the categories of no action, of unintentional act and of excusing circumstances. We have seen that the boundaries of these categories are often hard to draw because matters of degree are involved, and it is a matter of moral choice how much effort or self-sacrifice we think it reasonable to demand of people.

1 The standard doctrine appears in 'Freedom and Necessity' in his *Philosophical Essays*, 1954; the doubts are expressed in 'Fatalism' in his *The Concept of a Person*, 1963.
2 It has been characteristic of previous 'reconciliations' of determinism and moral responsibility that they have stressed that determinism does not make all blame ineffective, but have largely ignored the question of whether or not determinism makes all blame unjust. In this way, as well as in others, traditional soft determinism is incomplete.

But there is a more disturbing way in which the limits of a person's capacities can be hard to determine. Cases of no act or of unintentional act are relatively easy to identify, and there is considerable agreement as to their boundaries. As we have seen, greater problems arise over the point at which intentional acts should be excused because of circumstances limiting an agent's opportunities. And even harder problems are raised by the question of when an intentional act should be excused because of the agent's impaired capacities. The argument above, against the view that determinism entails that we are never capable of deciding differently from how we do decide, made use of the contrast between my capacity not to have a drink and the incapacity of the alcoholic. But, in order to substantiate the view that there is such a contrast, some indication must be given of its nature.

As long as the boundaries between those intentional actions that do and those that do not result from limited opportunities and impaired capacities are left unclear, people will be tempted to suppose that a causal explanation of an action is sufficient to show that the agent lacked the ability or opportunity to do anything else. It is sometimes held that a child is not responsible for what he does because his actions can be causally explained in terms of the type of upbringing he has had. Or again, 'he comes from a broken home' is often held to reduce the responsibility of a juvenile delinquent for what he has done, on the grounds that this has no doubt played an important causal role. Sometimes mental illness is thought of as absolving a person from responsibility because his actions are clearly caused by his disorder. And we are disinclined to hold anyone responsible for what he does as a result of a post-hypnotic suggestion, perhaps because we see the cause of his action. Similarly, many people would not want to hold the inhabitants of Brave New World responsible for what they do, since all their actions can be causally explained in terms of the environment and genetic make-up with which their rulers have supplied them.

But, if we are not to count the mere fact of causal explanation as an excuse, all these views as they stand are inadequate. The special problems raised by children, the mentally ill and the inhabitants of Brave New World concern intentional actions that are not done as the result of threats, torture or extreme need. Hence they concern cases where the excuses listed in the previous chapter do not apply. It may be that there are grounds for saying that these classes of people should not be held responsible for what they do. But this has to be argued for, by showing that their opportunities are limited or their abilities impaired in ways not so far considered. The mere fact that we can identify the most important causes of the actions in question is not a sufficient justification. There is a substantial recent philosophical literature devoted to the question of what it is to have the power to do something.[1] The strategy of the later chapters of this book is to approach the problem obliquely, by framing a question to put to psychiatrists about impairment of capacities. For the central problem posed by determinism is this: if we absolve some people from blame or punishment on account of their limited opportunities or capacities, what are the criteria of impaired ability that, in a determinist world, are satisfied by them but not by everyone else?

1   E.g. J. L. Austin, 'Ifs and Cans', *Proceedings of the British Academy, 1956,* and in *Philosophical Papers, 1961*; A. M. Honoré, 'Can and Can't', *Mind, 1964*; Stuart Hampshire, *Freedom of the Individual, 1965*; M. R. Ayers, *The Refutation of Determinism, 1968.*

5

CONSCIENCE AND CAPACITIES

It has been argued that determinism may well be true and that, even if it is not proved true, we would be misguided to base our reactions to people's conduct on the assumption that particular actions are uncaused. For there are insuperable logical difficulties in the attempt to establish that an action is uncaused. Whether or not the arguments of chapter two are taken to have dealt with the logical problems of proving that all events are caused, these problems are nothing to those confronting someone trying to prove that some particular event is uncaused. So it is true even in our present state of knowledge that, if moral blame presupposes that the blameworthy act is uncaused we can never justify blaming anyone for anything he does. We cannot be justified in any attitudes to people or actions that could not be held by a determinist.

But there are familiar disputes as to which attitudes are compatible with determinism. 'Hard' determinists claim that the truth of determinism undermines presuppositions that are essential to our whole attitudes of moral praise and blame, and that these attitudes must therefore be abandoned. Arguments have been given in support of the view that hard determinism can be rejected. 'Soft' determinists claim that our attitudes of moral praise and blame do not presuppose the falsity of determinism, and can therefore be retained. I have argued in favour of this view, but suggested that, as usually stated, it is incomplete. This lack of completeness consists in part in an unsatisfactory account of why we are justified in accepting that some factors excuse while some do not. Soft determinists normally discuss the question of when blame is effective, but ignore the question of when blame is fair or just. The previous chapter was an attempt to start filling in the gap. But the normal arguments for soft determinism are also incomplete in another way. It is claimed that, despite the truth of determinism, we can still distinguish between a case where someone had the physical and psychological power to do something other than he did, and a case where he did not have this power. The idea of something being in one's physical power is perhaps relatively clear, but the concept of psychological power is much less so. Unless a satisfactory account of the distinction between normal and impaired abilities of a psychological kind is provided, it is open to the hard determinist to claim that determinism places all courses of action except one outside our power.

There are intentional acts, other than those performed in excusing circumstances such as under threats or torture, or under pressure of extreme need, for which it is not reasonable to hold the agent responsible. These are intentional acts (including omissions) which are the result of impaired capacities. Some of the main abilities in question are of central importance to our idea of conscience. In this chapter, I shall argue that what it is to have a conscience, or be a moral agent, can best be understood as, among other things, the possession of certain abilities. And it is in this context that psychological incapacities can perhaps best be studied.

It may well not be possible to produce a morally 'neutral' account of the capacities necessary for being a moral agent, since it seems likely that different moral systems will to some extent demand different abilities from their adherents. But, in our own society, there is a cluster of phenomena that can loosely be grouped together under the heading of 'conscience'. It is said that psychopaths have no conscience, or that they are not moral agents. Part of the problem of psychopathy is to see what this can mean.

1 'GUILT RESPONSE' THEORIES OF CONSCIENCE

In a society where morality is widely held to be based on religious commands, a man's conscience can naturally be seen as a means of communication between God and himself, by which he becomes aware of divine approval or disapproval of his actions. Conscience is the inner voice that tells me what I ought to do, or alternatively the invisible eye of God that watches each move I make. But in a secular morality, these images do not help to answer some of the questions that suggest themselves about conscience. If morality has no religious basis, conscience seems to stand in need both of justification and of explanation. There is the perhaps empty question 'Why ought I to obey my conscience?' and there is also the causal question 'How do I come to have a conscience at all?'

The question of why one ought to obey one's conscience is either vacuous or else a genuine moral question, according to the interpretation placed on it. On one interpretation, to obey my conscience is simply to do what I ought to do, and then the question 'Why ought I to obey my conscience?' becomes a trivial one. It is a truism that I ought to do what I ought to do. But on another interpretation, the question is not trivial at all. If obeying one's conscience is not merely doing what one ought to do, but is rather doing what one *thinks* one ought to do, then the answer is less clear. Here, 'obeying one's conscience' is acting on one's own judgment in moral matters rather than obeying the moral advice or rules given by some other person or institution. Understood in this way, it becomes an open question whether or not one should always obey one's conscience. To this question, some traditional Protestant doctrines give opposite answers to some traditional Catholic doctrines. But it is worth mentioning that even where a man believes that he should subordinate his own conscience to the law or to the views of some church or political movement, this in turn is a moral belief of his, and so in one sense even here he is acting on his own conscience. Where I hold that some person or institution has a special moral authority such that I ought to obey their commands, I am taking on their moral views as mine, and the decision to do this is a moral act of mine for which, under normal conditions, I am responsible.

The question 'How do I come to have a conscience?' raises problems that are empirical rather than moral. The most influential attempt by a psychologist to give a causal account of the development of conscience is that of Freud. For him, as for Hobbes, man is not born a social animal, but enters the world with instincts that are dangerous to others unless they are restrained. He talks of 'the many developments, repressions, sublimations, and reaction-formations by means of which a child with a quite other innate endowment grows into what we call a normal man, the bearer, and in part the victim, of the civilization that has been so painfully acquired'.[1] Part of this painful process is when 'external compulsion is gradually internalized, in that a special mental function, man's superego, takes it under its jurisdiction. Every child presents to us the model of this transformation; it is only by that means that it becomes a moral and social being.'[2] During the Oedipus phase, when the young boy falls in love with his mother, his father is seen as an obstacle to the gratification of his desires, which then have to be repressed. 'So his infantile ego fortified itself for the carrying out of the repression by erecting this same obstacle within itself. . . . The superego retains the character of the father.'[3] The child internalizes his father's disapproval and feels guilty when he does anything he feels his father might not like. On Freud's view, this response of guilt to some of our actions then stays with us as long as we live, helping to preserve society by inhibiting the free play of our instincts.

It is often held that a psychoanalytic explanation of this kind is at the opposite extreme from the kind of explanation suggested by learning theory in experimental psychology. A psychologist such as Professor Eysenck, whose account of the development of conscience is based on the experimental evidence about conditioning and learning accumulated since the work of Pavlov, is unlikely to invoke the Oedipus complex as part of his theory. Eysenck distinguishes between learning and conditioning.[4] Learning is the process whereby pleasurable activities are remembered and activities that do not give pleasure are not. In learning to ride a bicycle, every correct movement gives the pleasure of achievement and so we remember how to repeat it. Conditioning, on the other hand, does not involve the voluntary repetition of what gives pleasure, but rather the sort of mechanical association

1 *Five Lectures on Psychoanalysis,* 1909. Standard Edition of the *Complete Works,* Vol. XI, p. 36.
2 *The Future of an Illusion,* 1927, Ch. 2.
3 *The Ego and the Id,* 1923, Ch. 3.
4 *Crime and Personality,* 1964, Ch. 5.

of stimulus and response that Pavlov obtained in his dogs. As an example of human conditioning, Eysenck cites J. B. Watson's successful attempt to induce a fear of rats in an eleven-month-old boy called Albert. Whenever Albert tried to play with his white rats, Watson struck a metal bar with a hammer, making a loud and frightening noise behind Albert's head.[1] After this had happened several times, Albert developed a strong fear of the rats. Eysenck draws a parallel between this process and the effects of punishing small children when they do things of which their elders disapprove. He says that children acquire 'a repertoire of conditional fear responses to a wide set of different behaviour patterns', and says that the responses of the autonomic nervous system when a person tells a lie suggest that such responses, 'conditioned according to ordinary Pavlovian conditioning, form the basis of what we would normally call our conscience'. He concludes that 'Conscience is indeed a conditioned reflex!'

Although there are clearly great differences between the theories of Freud and Eysenck, they have in common the assumption that conscience is a matter of certain kinds of emotional response mechanically being triggered off by situations associated with previous disapproval or punishment. To act on one's conscience is not seen as in any way involving rationality or deliberation. This assumption rests on too simple an account of the phenomena to be explained: on a failure to distinguish between different uses of the word 'conscience'. We often talk of 'pangs of conscience' or of a person having 'a guilty conscience', and here we are often alluding to the kind of emotional response that could be understood in terms of the Freud-Eysenck type of explanation. But we also talk of acting or of refusing to act as being on grounds of conscience, and we talk of 'obeying one's conscience'. This last expression is often equivalent in meaning to 'doing what one believes one ought to'. The reference in such cases is normally to a belief rather than to an emotional response, and beliefs about what one ought to do, like any other beliefs, can perfectly well be reached by a process of rational deliberation. We see the workings of conscience in the mental struggles of Cardinal Newman no less than in the behaviour of laboratory dogs.

1 Does 'the pursuit of knowledge' justify this experiment, or excuse it? Or neither?

Overlooking this distinction has led to over-simple explanations of the origins of conscience. It is not clear that our beliefs
about what we ought to do are to be explained in the same way
as our feelings of guilt. And it is not clear even that the emotional
responses associated with conscience are all to be explained in the
same way. Are my feelings when I am about to do something I
think wrong the same as the guilt feelings I have after doing it?
And even if they are, will the causal explanation be the same?
And are not my feelings in either of these cases perhaps different
from my feelings with respect to an action that I do not now
believe to be wrong, but which I had been brought up to think
wicked? Are the feelings associated with failure to do a good
action the same as those associated with doing something I think
is wrong? Will one explanation do for a person's emotional
reactions both to his bad acts and to his good acts?

Whatever the answers to these questions about our emotional
reactions, it is surely clear that our beliefs about what we ought
to do cannot be explained merely in terms of conditioned reflexes.
The term 'conditioned reflex' is very imprecise in meaning, but
presumably to say that something is a conditioned reflex is to
say more than just that it can be causally explained. To describe
what someone does as a conditioned reflex must at least be to
say that it could not have been altered by his own deliberation.
All the standard examples of unconditioned reflexes, such as the
reflex jerk of the leg when one's knee is tapped, as well as those of
conditioned reflexes given by experimental psychologists, share
this common feature. And the agent's impotence to alter his
reflexes by deliberation is a necessary condition of the success of
'lie detectors'. Since we often do alter our moral beliefs as a
result of deliberation, it cannot be true that all cases of acting on
moral beliefs are cases of acting merely as a result of conditioned
reflexes.

The deficiencies of crudely mechanical views of conscience
reflect the weaknesses of a crudely mechanical general theory of
the mind which is sometimes found in modern psychology, and
which has a distinguished history. When Hume said that 'Reason
is, and ought only to be the slave of the passions',[1] he was
expressing a view that underlies much modern theorizing about
motivation and 'drives'. This view has it that deliberation is of

1 *Treatise of Human Nature,* Book 2, Part 3, Section 3.

means, while our ends are determined by our nature. If I am hungry, I can reason about the best means of obtaining food, but I cannot reason about whether or not to desire it. Rational criticism can only be applied to desires when they are dependent upon false beliefs, as when I desire to eat the cold chicken in the refrigerator, not realizing that it has already been eaten by someone else. Otherwise rational objections are only appropriate if they are made to the means I choose to bring about the end I desire. As Hume provocatively puts it, ''Tis not contrary to reason to prefer the destruction of the whole world to the scratching of my finger.'[1]

The antithesis of this Humean doctrine is Kant's belief in the rational will. For Kant, 'the will is a faculty to choose that only which reason independent on inclination recognizes as practically necessary, i.e. as good'.[2] On this account, ends can be dictated either by inclinations, which are similar to Hume's 'passions', or else dictated by reason alone. Hume's view of the subservient role of reason makes him resort to an account of conscience in terms of a moral sense, so that we discern that an action is virtuous by the particular kind of pleasure it gives us. Kant rejects any appeal to a moral sense, and insists that genuine principles of morality are rational and quite independent of any inclination.

The disagreement between Hume and Kant is of a kind familiar in the history of philosophy, in which one half-truth is often opposed to another. Hume is correct in thinking that reason alone cannot supply a motive for an action, but incorrect in suggesting that the ends that we desire escape rational criticism altogether. The case for the view that reason alone cannot motivate actions can crudely be summed up in the slogan that deductive arguments must have premises. The conclusion of a deductive argument cannot provide us with any motive for action that was not implicitly contained in the premises.[3] Deductive reasoning may tell me that if I want good food I should avoid a certain restaurant, but, except where this is a means to some further end, no reasoning can tell me that good food is what I want.

But it is naïve to suppose that the ends one desires are beyond

1 *Ibid.*
2 *Fundamental Principles of the Metaphysic of Ethics,* translated by Abbott.
3 I do not wish to suggest that all reasoning is deductive.

rational criticism. At the simplest level, it is possible to abandon some end as a result of noticing its incompatibility with some other end which one considers more important. I may give up my desire for a fast car if I discover that its price makes buying such a car incompatible with other expensive desires that I mind about more. And since this kind of elementary economics textbook example does so little justice to the complexity of most real situations involving incompatible ends, the role of reasoning in such real cases is correspondingly less trivial. This is not merely a matter of the difficulty of assigning relative importance to different ends, or of the calculations being more complex than simple monetary ones. It is often a matter of one's ends being of radically different types. A man can have a number of different things he would like to have or to do, but realize that if too many of these ends were realized he would become the sort of person he does not wish to be. ('Yes, it would be nice to live by the Mediterranean and not have to work, but do I really want to be a rich and idle expatriate?') Or again, more clearly relevant to an account of conscience, one can come to realize that, in some cases where one's aims come into conflict with those of other people, to realize one's personal aims is incompatible with more general aims one has for people at large.

When we make an appeal to someone's conscience, we are often trying to persuade them to reason in this way about their ends. Moral exhortation often takes the form of saying things like 'If you treat her like that you will make her very unhappy', where the speaker presupposes that the person he is addressing has the general aim of avoiding making people unhappy. The ability to subject one's aims to rational criticism and appraisal, and the ability to modify them accordingly, are factors relevant to the distinction between someone capable of acting on his conscience and someone who merely has the ability to obey those rules that pass as 'moral' in a given community. Piaget's study[1] of conscience in children suggests that a large part of a child's moral development consists in the transition from obeying learned rules to a stage of greater autonomy, when obedience is no longer an unquestioned end in itself, but the rules are instead themselves subjected to criticism.

But if an appeal to someone's conscience is often a more rational

[1] *The Moral Judgement of the Child,* 1932.

matter than an attempt to elicit a conditioned reflex, it is also often as much an appeal to the imagination as to reason. The imagination is not much discussed in psychology, partly no doubt because of its apparent elusiveness as a field of study. It is easier to devise psychological tests for extraversion than for imaginativeness, and mental images are notoriously inaccessible to precise scientific investigation. And recent philosophical discussions of the imagination have been both rare[1] and excessively narrow. Both Ryle[2] and Sartre[3] write as if the imagination consisted almost entirely in the capacity to visualize some object not present. But an imaginative man is not merely someone who has the capacity to conjure up mental images. It is surely a commonplace that one can use one's imagination in producing an original scientific theory, in writing a poem, or in drawing up a political programme.

The ways in which imagination is connected with morality have little to do with mental images. Part of the development of moral sensitivity is the growing ability to realize that other people respond to situations in ways that are very similar to one's own responses. A child learns that bullying is wrong, not merely because the rules forbid it, but because other people dislike being hit as much as he does. This knowledge may be so familiar to most adults that its original acquisition does not seem the imaginative feat that perhaps it was. But some of the achievements of the moral imagination are far less commonplace. It is easy for us to be aware of the extent to which our next door neighbour minds about misfortune, but far less easy to appreciate what it is like to be a hungry man in India or China. And even in face to face relationships, some people are better than others at discerning the extent to which their friends' feelings and responses resemble or do not resemble their own.

To appeal to someone's conscience is often to ask them to make an effort of imagination. The moral education of adults has often had to repeat the process by which children learn that other people as much as themselves have needs, desires and the capacity to be hurt. But for most adults, it is only special classes of people

1 Although the relevance of imagination to morality is not ignored in Professor R. M. Hare's *Freedom and Reason*, 1963.
2 *The Concept of Mind*, 1949, Ch. 8.
3 *The Psychology of Imagination*, 1940.

with respect to whom this imaginative effort has to be made. One of the functions of literature and art can be to extend our imagination by showing us alternative ways of seeing the world and of responding to people. At various times, moral reformers have had to argue that slaves, criminals and the insane have feelings and responses similar to those of other men and should be treated accordingly. The sort of imaginative grasp that is relevant has been described by Tolstoy in a passage in *Anna Karenina*:

> Levin had often noticed in discussions between the most intelligent people that, after enormous efforts and endless logical subtleties and talk, the disputants finally became aware that what they had been at such pains to prove to one another had long ago, from the beginning of the argument, been known to both, but that they liked different things, and would not define what they liked for fear of its being attacked. He had often had the experience of suddenly, in the middle of a discussion grasping what it was the other liked, and at once liking it too, and immediately found himself agreeing, and then all arguments fell away useless.

2 HOLDING MORAL BELIEFS

No doubt the phenomena of 'conscience' are too loosely grouped together for a rigid definition of the word in terms of necessary and sufficient conditions to be helpful. Having a conscience is not an all-or-none affair, and we talk of someone's conscience being well developed or not. It is plausible that our thinking that someone has a well developed conscience is not related merely to his responses of guilt, but also to the extent to which his capacities of imagination and of reasoning are developed. Yet it would be odd to ascribe a conscience to someone who, while both rational and imaginative, held no moral beliefs at all. Having a conscience is not merely the possession of capacities, but also involves having moral views about what one ought to do. It is desirable to have some way of deciding whether or not someone holds a moral belief.

How can we tell whether or not someone really holds the moral belief he professes? The importance of distinguishing between someone who genuinely believes in a moral principle and a hypocrite who merely says that he does makes it tempting to support a kind of 'moral behaviourism', whereby deeds, not words, become the criterion of real moral belief. This temptation is to suggest that a person can correctly be said to hold a moral principle only if he at least usually acts upon it when a relevant situation presents itself. This view makes it possible to state the difference between a sincere and an insincere profession of a moral principle, but has the disadvantage of making it very hard to account for cases where someone shows great weakness of will. In such cases it seems possible for someone genuinely to hold that he ought, say, to give up smoking or to write frequent letters to his relations, and yet persistently fail to act on his belief. It seems wrong to classify moral weakness with hypocrisy, by denying that such a man can really hold the belief.

One way out of this difficulty has been proposed by Professor Hare,[1] who says that 'the typical case of moral weakness, as opposed to that of hypocrisy, is a case of "ought but can't"'. Hare's criterion of sincerity he expresses as follows: 'It is a tautology to say that we cannot sincerely assent to a command addressed to ourselves, and at the same time not perform it, if now is the occasion for performing it, and it is in our (physical and psychological) power to do so.'[2] He plausibly argues that the passage in which St Paul says 'The good which I want to do, I fail to do; but what I do is the wrong which is against my will' is one that in context suggests that it was not in his psychological power to act differently. This criterion has the advantage of giving us a way of distinguishing between a weak willed man and a hypocrite, for the former has not the power to act on his principle while the latter has that power. Hare appears to make this distinction the basis of a definition of hypocrisy, for he says, 'Nor will it do to quote cases in which a man goes on saying that he ought, but fails to act, even though he can act, in every sense of "can". For this is the case of what I called purposive backsliding, or hypocrisy; and these are allowed for.'

1   *Op. cit.*, p. 80.
2   *The Language of Morals*, 1952, p. 20. Difficulties in Hare's view have been discussed, e.g. in Gardiner, 'On Assenting to a Moral Principle', *Proceedings of the Aristotelian Society*, 1954–5, and in Lukes, 'Moral Weakness', *Philosophical Quarterly*, 1965.

It is not clear what is the force of a claim that someone can act 'in every sense' of 'can' unless one specifies all the different senses of that word. But it seems plausible that Hare means that the man in question has not only the opportunity and physical ability to act, but also that psychological power that St Paul is said to have lacked. But the concept of 'psychological power' is not a clear one. How do we tell whether or not it is within someone's psychological power to do something? Presumably the fact that he does not do it is not sufficient to show that it was not in his psychological power, for this would entail that, on Hare's definition, there is no such thing as hypocrisy. But what alternative criteria are there? If we say that something is not in my psychological power where I try to do it, but fail, this in turn presents problems. In the first place, one must restrict the nature of the failure that is relevant, so that failure resulting from external interference does not count as evidence of my limited psychological power. But even in a case where I try to make myself get up out of bed, and fail although no one else prevents me from getting up, is it clear that it was not in my psychological power to do better than this? What reply can I make to the person who says, 'It was in your psychological power: you just did not try hard enough'? If the reply is that it was not in my psychological power to try harder, it is again unclear how this could be established. One way of establishing this would be to invoke that plea of 'he could not do (or try) otherwise' that is entailed by determinism, but, if this were what were meant by 'power', the truth of determinism would entail that I never have the psychological power to do anything that I do not in fact do. This argument again rules out the possibility of Hare's criterion of hypocrisy ever being satisfied.

These difficulties can be avoided if we abandon Hare's insistence that a man who says that he ought to do something, but does not do it, must either be unable to do it or else be a hypocrite. The distinction between two uses of the word 'conscience' has been emphasized here. On one use, to have a conscience is to be prone to feelings of guilt or remorse. On another use, it is among other things to have beliefs about what one ought to do. But these two uses of the word are not entirely unrelated. Proneness to feelings of guilt or remorse is evidence relevant to deciding whether or not a man genuinely holds certain moral beliefs about what he ought to do. Just as one can hold a moral belief and yet sometimes not act on it, so the links between failure to act on one's beliefs and guilt feelings are not rigid either. One can feel guilty, perhaps as a result of childhood conditioning, without going against one's present beliefs. One can also fail to act on one's beliefs without feeling guilty. But, nonetheless, if a man feels guilty when he does not act on a principle, this is evidence in favour of the view that it really is one of his principles.

One reservation must be made here. A hypocrite may sometimes feel remorseful or guilty on account of his hypocrisy. If a man tries to create a good impression by insincerely saying that he believes in giving away a quarter of his income, he may afterwards feel guilty about his pretence. This guilt is evidence, not that he really does believe in such generosity, but rather that he disapproves of hypocrisy.

It may be objected that feelings of guilt are not much help in showing that someone holds a moral belief, since a determined hypocrite can pretend to a guilt he does not feel. But it is only claimed that behaviour indicating feelings of guilt is evidence of sincerity. It is always possible to doubt someone's sincerity, but this doubt becomes more unreasonable as evidence of sincerity accumulates.

3 PSYCHOLOGICAL INCAPACITY

Where a man has some mental illness, brain damage or chemical abnormality, his condition may be such that his actions cannot be altered by persuasion. This may be because he is unable to alter his intentions in response to argument, or because, if he does alter his intentions, he will be unable to act upon them. This brings to light another plea that can be made by the expression 'he could not help it', and be used to excuse someone from responsibility for what he did. So far, we have only distinguished one kind of plea that excuses intentional acts: that of excusing circumstances (such as a situation involving threats, torture or extreme need). But it is surely reasonable to accept that someone could not help his intentional act if his intention was one that he was incapable of altering.

The analysis of this type of case, which can be called one of

97

'unalterable intention', is helpful for Hare's problem of distinguishing between weakness of will and hypocrisy. As we saw, Hare says that if we really hold a moral belief, but do not act upon it when we know it to be relevant, then acting on it at that moment must be outside either our physical or our psychological power. But he gives no account of what it means to say that something is or is not within one's psychological power. If an account can be given of 'unalterable intention' such that we can discriminate between those who cannot act on their belief and those who can but do not, we will be able to avoid the paradoxical claim that all cases of weakness of will are cases of incapacity.

It may be objected that a plea of unalterable intention is merely a version of the plea of causal explanation, which we have rejected as an excuse. And, if determinism is true, the existence of a causal explanation will fail to be a distinguishing feature of any particular subclass of cases. But a case of unalterable intention is not merely one where the agent's intention can be causally explained.

This kind of case differs from normal cases of intentional action in that the agent is not open to persuasion to alter his intention. If I intend to have another drink before going home, you may be able to persuade me to change my mind, perhaps by reminding me that I am driving, or by giving me reasons why I should go at once. But if an alcoholic intends to have another drink before going home, persuading him to change his mind may be a hopeless task, since he cannot in this respect control himself. This is not because his intention can be causally explained and mine cannot. There seems no reason to suppose that my intention is uncaused, although the causal explanation may well differ in the two cases. The test for self-control, which differentiates between my intention and that of the alcoholic, is that my intention can be altered by providing reasons that give me a sufficiently strong motive, while his can only be altered, if at all, by some form of manipulation such as behaviour therapy or drugs. And this impotence of reasons applies whether they are put forward by other people or by the alcoholic himself. When a drink is not available, such a person may sometimes convince himself of the undesirability of having one, but when it becomes available again his intention to have it will simply re-assert itself. Where we have evidence of an unalterable intention of this kind, it is reasonable to say that the person who acts on it cannot help what he does.

There is no sharp boundary between the states of being and not being open to persuasion. A man is not one day merely a heavy drinker and the next day an alcoholic. But because 'unalterable intention' is a matter of degree, this does not mean that this plea should not be accepted as excusing from responsibility. We have seen that even the involuntariness of a movement is a matter of degree, and yet we do not hesitate to excuse people where their movements were involuntary. When someone claims in court that his stealing was a manifestation of kleptomania, he is implying that his is a case of unalterable intention. The traditional legal question, 'Would he have done it with a policeman standing at his elbow?' has been subjected to much well-deserved criticism, but it is important to recognize that the question is not mistaken in principle. The question is clearly designed to see whether he was open to persuasion, for the threat posed by the presence of the policeman is a powerful reason for him to give up his intention of stealing. As such, it is trying to elicit the right kind of information: it is only absurd because it postulates such powerful persuasion. An alcoholic might well not have his other drink with a policeman at his elbow (if, say, it were after closing time) but the fact that he can be influenced by such strong and crude pressures does not show that under normal circumstances he is able to resist drinking. And the same may well hold for the kleptomaniac and his stealing. Being tall is a matter of degree, and any boundary between tall people and others will be largely arbitrary. But if, for some purpose, we wished to select all tall people, it might well be foolish to make seven foot six inches the dividing line.

One's intention is unalterable where one is not open to being persuaded by reasons to alter it. Here 'reasons' should not be thought of narrowly (perhaps as merely being valid deductive arguments) but broadly as being grounds for acting. This is not to say that one has some psychological incapacity whenever one is presented with reasons for changing one's course of action and yet does not do so. The reasons may not be good ones, or they may be outweighed by better ones. I only suffer from a psychological incapacity of this kind when I am not open to persuasion by reasons which fall into one of two classes. They may be reasons which I myself accept as being sufficiently good to make me change my mind if I were able to, as when the alcoholic admits that he would be better off if he gave up drinking. Or they may be reasons which, one has adequate grounds for saying, would be so accepted by the person in question if he were able to reason properly, or were not in some way deluded.

A drug addict who is in a state of appalling suffering, and certain to die as a result of his condition, may refuse to recognize that he would be better off if he were cured. But the avoidance of suffering and the saving of one's life are reasons such that in these circumstances we can only suppose they are ignored as the result of some delusion or inability to reason. It seems preposterous to deny that the addict is unable to give up the drug, on the grounds that he does not accept the reasons for doing so. But we are not entitled to say that anyone who does not respond to our persuasion about anything has some psychological incapacity. People quite legitimately differ as to how much weight to give to different reasons in deciding between courses of action. The grounds for saying that a reason or set of reasons are so good that their rejection must result from delusion or incapacity have to be very strong. The type of evidence relevant includes facts about the person being harmed and yet unaware of this. The problem of when we are entitled to claim that someone is unconsciously harmed will be discussed in Chapter 6.

When we consider someone who knowingly breaks one of his own principles, where it is in his physical power not to do so, we are not always forced to say that he had some psychological incapacity. If, like the alcoholic or the drug addict, he is not open to persuasion by himself or by other people, then he does have a psychological incapacity. Yet, if a reasonable amount of persuasion would alter his intention, but he himself chooses to avert his attention from the reasons in question, his is then a case of moral weakness without psychological incapacity. If so, under normal circumstances, there is no reason to absolve him from responsibility for what he does.

The example of an alcoholic shows that there is a middle position between being and not being a responsible agent in general. Perhaps some severe types of mental illness are such that those suffering from them behave in a way that cannot in any respect be altered by a reasonable degree of persuasion. But an alcoholic is not in this position. He may be quite open to persuasion where any action not connected with his desire for drink is concerned. It is only with regard to one pattern of behaviour that his intentions are unalterable.

6

THE CONCEPT OF MENTAL ILLNESS

In this Act 'mental disorder' means mental illness, arrested
or incomplete development of mind, psychopathic disorder,
and any other disorder or disability of mind; and 'mentally
disordered' shall be construed accordingly.

From *The Mental Health Act,* 1959

A clear and complete insight into the nature of madness, a
correct and distinct conception of what constitutes the
difference between the sane and the insane has, as far as I
know, not as yet been found.

Schopenhauer: *The World as Will and Idea*

The most perplexing legal problems about a man's responsibility
for what he does are raised in cases that hinge on questions of
mental illness. Should certain kinds of mental illness absolve
people from legal responsibility for their actions? If so, how
should the law distinguish between those kinds of disorder that
excuse and those that do not? And how can courts be sure that
someone genuinely is mentally ill? Mental illness raises legal
problems more acutely than does physical illness, in part because
mental disorder is more often associated with crime than is
physical disorder. But a far more important reason for these legal
perplexities is the obscurity in which the whole subject of mental
illness is still shrouded. We are so far from having adequate

explanations of mental illness that it is hard to be sure that our classifications of it have much value. And some psychiatrists have even suggested that to talk of mental 'illness' at all may merely be to use a misleading metaphor.

I DOUBTS ABOUT THE CONCEPT OF MENTAL ILLNESS

Several critics have suggested that mental illness is a myth,[1] or, more moderately, that the criteria of mental illness are not sufficiently precise or objective. In her discussion of this concept, Lady Wootton[2] says that prevailing views of mental disorder and its role in anti-social behaviour rest on the proposition that 'mental health and its correlative, mental illness, are objective in the sense that they are more than an expression either of the tastes and value-judgments of psychiatrists, or of the cultural norms of a particular society: mental health is to be regarded as closely analogous to, and no less real than, its physical counterpart'. She goes on to quote various psychiatrists whose attempts to support this view by providing objective criteria of mental health and illness go a long way towards undermining it. Among her quotations are the following:

> The well adjusted personality, which characterizes a happy and efficient man or woman, is a harmonious blending of these varied emotions and character traits, resulting in self-control and habits of conformity.

> A mature and mentally healthy person is one who . . . (and) carries on his work, play, and his family and social life with confidence and enthusiasm and with a minimum of conflict, fear and hostility.

> Let us define mental health as the adjustment of human beings to the world and to each other with a maximum of effectiveness and happiness. Not just efficiency, or just

1 Szasz, *The Myth of Mental Illness*, 1961.
2 *Social Science and Social Pathology*, 1959, Ch. 7. Lady Wootton's arguments concerning two specific varieties of disorder are criticized by Haksar, 'The Responsibility of Mental Defectives', *Philosophy*, 1963, and 'The Responsibility of Psychopaths', *Philosophical Quarterly*, 1965.

contentment – or the grace of obeying the rules of the game cheerfully. It is all of these together. It is the ability to maintain an even temper, an alert intelligence, socially considerate behaviour, and a happy disposition. This, I think, is a healthy mind.

Mental health consists of the ability to live . . . happily, productively, without being a nuisance.

In my work in other fields, my co-workers and I have settled for some such simple criteria as these: the ability to hold a job, have a family, keep out of trouble with the law, and enjoy the usual opportunities for pleasure.

Wholesome-minded people are not averse to frank consideration of sex under proper conditions and right motives, but they do not enjoy having it dragged into prominence on every possible pretext and occasion. Dignity and decency are the marks of successful sex adjustment.

Industrial unrest to a large degree means bad mental hygiene, and is to be corrected by good mental hygiene.

These people of happy disposition and conformist habits, full of dignity and decency, who are never a nuisance and never upset their employers or the police, may excite the admiration of some psychiatrists. It is hard to see that they alone satisfy some evaluatively neutral medical criteria for mental health. Lady Wootton rightly criticizes these accounts as being tied to the values of a specific culture, and points out that on some of these definitions a sadist might be considered to be in perfect mental health, as might a Nazi in a Nazi-run society. Even if one does not share Lady Wootton's objection to definitions that do not include Nazis among the mentally ill, one may reasonably feel uneasy about another consequence of some of those same definitions: that all liberals in a Nazi society are mentally ill.

Lady Wootton goes on to cite instances such as that of a man in the United States who, on learning from a cab driver that what he most wanted in life was to own his own cab, gave him five thousand dollars; as a result of this he was sent to a mental hospital. She also quotes two psychiatrists who used the fact that a woman was starting on her fourth marriage as evidence of her 'neurotic make-up'. She suggests that, since no scientifically neutral definition of mental illness has been provided, we should look with great suspicion on the attempt to assimilate mental to physical disorders and to treat both alike. She also takes the view that we should distrust attempts to excuse anti-social behaviour by pointing to mental illness, where the behaviour in question is the only evidence for the illness.

Some sociological studies[1] of psychiatric treatment claim to show that in some communities there is a larger ratio of neurotics to psychotics among those in the higher social classes having treatment than there is among those in the lower social classes having treatment. It is possible that the higher one's social class the greater is the danger of neurosis or the less the danger of psychosis. It is possible that the cost of treatment deters lower class neurotics from seeking treatment. But it is also possible that, even if either or both of these views are correct, the explanation may also lie partly in differences between what counts as mental illness in different social classes. It may be that behaviour that in one class is seen as symptomatic of a neurotic illness would not be seen as such in another class. Any studies that provide evidence in favour of this view will give support to Lady Wootton's criticisms of the relativism of much talk of mental illness.

Some reinforcement of those criticisms is provided by the studies of mental hospital life carried out by Professor Goffman.[2] He states some of his conclusions as follows:

> The student of mental hospitals can discover that the craziness or 'sick behaviour' claimed for the mental patient is by and large a product of the claimant's social distance from the situation that the patient is in, and is not primarily a product of mental illness. Whatever the refinements of the various patients' psychiatric diagnoses, and whatever the special ways in which social life on the 'inside' is unique, the researcher can find that he is participating in a community not significantly different from any other he has studied. Of course, while restricting himself to the off-ward grounds community of paroled patients, he may feel that chronic 'back' wards are socially crazy places. But he need

1 E.g. Hollingshead and Redlich, *Social Class and Mental Illness*, 1958.
2 *Asylums*, 1961.

only move his sphere of sympathetic participation to the
'worst' ward in the hospital, and this, too, can come into
social focus as a place with a liveable and continuously
meaningful social world.

Goffman does not express scepticism about the status of the
concept of mental illness itself, but his conclusions, if accepted,
cast doubt on some of the evidence used in support of the view
that a particular patient is in fact mentally ill. He suggests that
it is partly a matter of chance whether or not someone is seen as
being in need of going to a mental hospital, and that when one is
in such an institution one's apparently 'crazy' behaviour can often
be understood as a natural response to one's situation.

In support of his view that whether or not one ends up in a
mental hospital is partly a matter of chance, Goffman cites a
number of 'career contingencies' on which it depends, such as
social and economic status, visibility of the 'offence', proximity
to a mental hospital, the availability of treatment and the attitude
of the community to that treatment. He mentions other possible
career contingencies, such as when a rebellious adolescent
daughter is sent to a mental hospital, if she starts an open affair
with an unsuitable companion and can no longer be managed at
home. That there is a real possibility of this type of case is suggested by testimony given by Dr Braceland to the United States
Senate Subcommittee on the Constitutional Rights of the Mentally Ill. He said, 'If a man brings his daughter to me from California, because she is in manifest danger of falling into vice or
in some way disgracing herself, he doesn't expect me to let her
loose in my hometown for that same thing to happen.'[1]

Goffman considers that a great deal of the apparently extra-
ordinary behaviour of inmates of mental hospitals consists of
intelligible responses to features of the institutions within which
they find themselves. He draws attention to uncomfortably close
parallels between mental hospitals and other 'total institutions',
such as prisons, army camps, boarding schools, concentration
camps and monasteries. Many of these institutions have much in
common. Visits from the outside world are rare; on arrival there
are often what amount to degradation ceremonies, such as giving

[1] Quoted in Szasz: *Law, Liberty and Psychiatry*, 1963, which contains several
interesting case histories of 'false commitment' in the United States.

the new inmate a bath, replacing ordinary clothes by a uniform, hair-cutting or finger-printing; there is a rigid status hierarchy between staff and inmates; inmates are made to behave respectfully to staff and are often humiliated. Goffman does not suggest that the reasons advanced for the ways in which mental hospitals are run are never good ones, but his description of the similarities between different total institutions are sufficiently persuasive to make one suspect that some ways in which patients are treated are dictated by the needs of the institution rather than by medical science.

Goffman says that a patient will sometimes carry his blanket around with him during the day, and may curl up on the floor with his blanket completely covering him, and says that this sort of act is thought to be 'highly regressive'. But he suggests that such actions can be perfectly well understood in terms of their social context. In a community where people are deprived of status and of privacy, as well as of most of their control over their own lives, it is natural that there should develop an 'underlife', consisting of arrangements whereby 'a member of an organization employs unauthorized means, or obtains unauthorized ends, or both, thus getting around the organization's assumptions as to what he should do and get and hence what he should be'.[1] Part of this underlife may consist in the acquisition by the patient of 'personal territory', within which he develops tacit rights and feels some degree of privacy or protection. Some patients have private rooms; others may acquire rights to sit in particular chairs. But where in such a community one has acquired no such rights, to enclose a private region inside one's blanket may be the best one can do.

This behaviour with blankets is one of Goffman's numerous illustrations of his thesis that within mental hospitals a kind of vicious circle operates.[2] The hardships of the patients' situation cause them to respond in a way that appears to confirm the view that this situation is appropriate for them. A patient who is isolated and naked, without any other means of expression may

1   *Op. cit.,* p. 189.
2   These numerous illustrations of Goffman's thesis make it seem plausible, but they by no means establish its truth; nor is it clear how one could establish with certainty that Goffman's view of, say, the curling up in a blanket, was true.

be able to show his resentment only by tearing up his mattress or by writing with excrement on the wall. Such actions are seen as psychotic symptoms, and the authorities are unlikely to transfer the patient to a more pleasant part of the hospital. Throughout Goffman's enumeration of such examples runs the social anthropologist's view that forms of behaviour are functions of social systems, and one is left wondering whether our attitudes towards those in mental hospitals do not resemble the crudely 'superior' attitude taken by ignorant people to the practices of other societies.

Another, perhaps less cautious, scepticism about mental illness derives from the school of 'existentialist' psychiatry, one of whose foremost exponents in Britain is Dr R. D. Laing. The whole emphasis of this approach is on understanding the patient's predicament in his own terms, and Laing has written persuasive descriptions of how schizophrenics see themselves and their relationships with others.[1] He argues that the behaviour of schizophrenics is generally an intelligible response to the world as they see it, and can often be seen as being at least as rational as the actions of more 'normal' people. He has written:

> In the context of our present pervasive madness that we
> call normality, sanity, freedom, all our frames of reference
> are ambiguous and equivocal. A man who prefers to be dead
> rather than Red is normal. A man who says he has lost his
> soul is mad. A man who says that men are machines may
> be a great scientist. A man who says that he *is* a machine is
> 'depersonalized' in psychiatric jargon. A man who says that
> negroes are an inferior race may be widely respected. A man
> who says his whiteness is a form of cancer is certifiable. A
> little girl of seventeen in a mental hospital told me she was
> terrified because the Atom Bomb was inside her. That is a
> delusion. The statesmen of the world who boast and
> threaten that they have Doomsday weapons are far more
> dangerous, and far more estranged from 'reality' than many
> of the people on whom the label 'psychotic' is affixed.[2]

Laing argues that schizophrenic behaviour is a natural response to certain types of human situations, which result from the con-

1 *The Divided Self* (1960, Pelican edition 1965).
2 *Ibid.* Preface to 1965 edition.

tradictory demands made upon people by their relationships with others, especially members of their families. Having given a causal account of schizophrenia in terms of social and personal relationships, he goes on to describe schizophrenic experience as a 'voyage into inner space and time',[1] and says that 'we can no longer assume that such a voyage is an illness that has to be treated'.[2] He goes on to ask, 'Can we not see that this voyage is not what we need to be cured of, but that it is itself a natural way of healing our own appalling state of alienation called normality?'

It will be clear that Laing's approach is very different from the cool scepticism of Lady Wootton. But they both challenge the common view that some states of mind or some types of behaviour constitute 'mental illnesses', which are objectively identifiable by medical science, and from which it is desirable that people should be cured. This challenge can only properly be evaluated in the context of understanding the type of knowledge we have of the states of mind and behaviour that lead to psychiatric treatment.

2 STANDARDS FOR PSYCHIATRIC EXPLANATION

Present-day psychology and psychiatry can often seem to be in the state of scientific development of physics and astronomy before Aristotle. The Babylonians by patient observation had discovered regularities on the basis of which they could predict eclipses and other phenomena, but their discoveries did not give rise to any explanatory theory. The pre-Socratic philosophers, on the other hand, asked fundamental questions about the ultimate composition of the world, and put forward theories of great generality with no experimental support. Today the Babylonians are the experimental psychologists, who can tell us what conditions are favourable for extinguishing conditioned reflex eye blinks, or the psychiatrists who are unable to account for the success of their drugs in treating schizophrenics. And the modern pre-Socratics are the Freudians and other psychoanalytic theorists, who advance bold fundamental theories unhampered by any considerations of testability. If these parallels are even

1 *The Politics of Experience* (1967), p. 120.   2 *Ibid.*, p. 136.

partly just, it is understandable that there should be scepticism about even the most basic categories of psychiatry.

In order to give some idea of the standards to which psychiatric explanation should ideally aspire, one may take as an example the explanation of the type of feeble-mindedness known as phenylketonuria. This type of feeble-mindedness can normally be identified by the presence of large quantities of phenylpyruvic acid in the patients' urine. In normal people, phenylalanine is converted into phenylpyruvic acid, which is then turned into tyrosine. We now understand that phenylketonuria is caused by a block in this metabolic pathway so that the phenylpyruvic acid accumulates. This condition is inherited, and depends on a single recessive gene. It can be successfully treated by eliminating phenylalanine from the diet. Although the details of the links between the blocking of the metabolic pathway and the feeble-mindedness have not been traced, this explanation of phenylketonuria is far more satisfactory than most psychiatric explanations of mental illnesses. It provides an account of the origins of the disease, and gives us both a successful treatment and a reason why that treatment should work. If psychiatric treatments and explanations of the various mental illnesses conformed to these requirements, scepticism might seem merely foolish.

3 PSYCHIATRIC CLASSIFICATION OF NEUROSES AND PSYCHOSES

Various psychiatric textbooks differ in their vocabulary and in the ways in which they classify mental illnesses. But there is some agreement about the most general categories of disorder. There is most agreement about those disorders most obviously associated with some physical malfunctioning: mental deficiency, epilepsy, and the mental disorders associated with brain tumours, with brain infection or damage and with senility. These raise few conceptual problems. Other mental illnesses are often classified at the most general level into neuroses, psychoses and 'personality disorders'. Different writers draw the boundaries of this last term more or less widely, and those who interpret 'personality disorders' more narrowly accordingly have to enlarge their number of fundamental categories of disorder.

The types of symptom classified as neurotic include some states of depression and anxiety, compulsive habits such as hand-washing, exaggerated fears of particular things or situations, such as dogs or open spaces, and 'illness' that seems more a response to emotional stress than the result of any physical disorder. The states of anxiety and depression that count as neurotic either have no reason or else are very excessive reactions to whatever triggers them off. If one tries to define 'neurosis', it is tempting to say that a neurosis is a mental state or pattern of behaviour which the patient recognizes to be undesirable but which he cannot by himself eliminate. But this definition will not cover most cases of neurotic 'illness', where doctors say the pains have no physiological basis and are thus 'hysterical conversion symptoms'. In such a case, the patient will often fiercely deny that his symptoms are neurotic, and will not accept that they are indicative of an undesirable mental state.

Even to describe a symptom as 'hysterical' raises difficulties. It is hard to be sure that the symptoms have no physical cause. And the obscurity of the term 'hysteria' can be seen from any textbook account. Consider this one:[1]

> In British psychiatry it is usual to call those states hysterical in which some motivation for the symptoms can be discovered. The distinction between these states and those produced by malingering then becomes one of theoretical difficulty, and needs the postulation of an 'unconscious' in which in the hysteric the motivation lies submerged, or of some other hypothetical mechanism. In practice the hysteric is not infrequently a malingerer too; and patients are seen, whom all would call hysterical, where motivation remains speculative even after intensive enquiry. No definition so far framed covers all those and only those states which the clinician must call hysterical; and the category of hysteria is essentially a clinical one, to which a name can be given, but no logically satisfying definition.
>
> Hysteria can manifest itself in an innumerable number of forms, and in fact may mimic almost any disease. Not only

1 Mayer-Gross, Slater and Roth, *Clinical Psychiatry*, Second Edition, 1960. Since this chapter was written, Slater and Roth have brought out the Third Edition, 1969, in which it is admitted that the concept of 'hysteria' has been much criticized, but the passage quoted here is largely retained.

may any symptom whatsoever, physical or psychological, be hysterical in a particular case, but also well-marked hysterical traits can be seen which are not to be called symptoms. Some personalities succeed in giving even their smallest acts a hysterical quality, but nevertheless go through life without any form of mental illness.

The textbook goes on to say that 'the quality that emerges as the most plausible single feature constant to all cases is the tendency to dissociation, to a breakdown in central nervous integration'. This is expanded by reference to symptoms of physical diseases the patient does not have, or to the absence of emotional reaction to diseases he does have. Criticism of such an account is superfluous: quotation is enough.

If one turns from attempts to define 'neurosis', or individual neuroses, in terms of symptoms, it is natural to seek definitions in terms of causes. But here agreement seems very remote. Some psychiatrists stress anxiety as a prime cause of neurosis. Others, the 'behaviour therapists', stress 'over-learning'. Psycho-analysts lay emphasis on the Freudian theory of neuroses originating in childhood repression of the sexual instincts. Claims are made for the effectiveness of behaviour therapy in treating phobias and compulsive behaviour, and both for drugs and for electric shock treatment in dealing with depressive states. It seems unlikely that all the symptoms classified as 'neurotic' have sufficiently similar causes to give a basis for a definition. And even with particular kinds of symptom, such as phobias, no eclectic insistence on the multiplicity of causes seems likely to produce the psychiatric agreement needed for a causal classification of neuroses.

The diagnosis of 'psychosis' is much less unclear than that of 'neurosis'. There is general agreement that psychosis involves either having delusions or at least that 'the psychopathological way of living is, in a certain way, accepted by the patient. Unlike the psychoneurotic, the psychotic does not fight his disorder.'[1]

A common classification of psychoses distinguishes between those that are organic and those that are functional. Organic psychoses are those for which a physiological basis has been discovered, while functional psychoses are those with no known

[1] Arieti, in the *American Handbook of Psychiatry*, 1959.

physiological basis. Despite its frequent occurrence in psychiatric literature, this distinction is widely seen to be unsatisfactory, for it is based on our relative ignorance. We have no proof of the existence of a special class of mental disorders without physiological basis.

An alternative classification of psychoses distinguishes between affective, paranoid and schizophrenic psychoses. Affective psychoses consist of those depressive, manic and manic-depressive states that are sufficiently severe to involve delusions or hallucinations, and so are excluded from the class of neuroses. Paranoid psychoses involve delusions of persecution and an attitude of suspicion. The third main variety of psychosis, schizophrenia, is far less easy to characterize.

A typical account of schizophrenia is the following:

One of a group of psychotic reactions, often beginning after adolescence or in young adulthood, characterized by fundamental disturbances in reality relationships and concept formations, with associated affective, behavioural and intellectual disturbances in varying degrees and mixtures. These reactions are marked by a tendency to withdraw from reality, inappropriate moods, unpredictable disturbances in stream of thought, regressive tendencies to the point of deterioration, and often hallucinations and delusions.[1]

When confronted with such an account, it is reasonable to wonder if this cluster of 'disturbances in varying degrees and mixtures' forms a unitary condition at all. But most writers insist that there is a recognizable syndrome, although there are different varieties of schizophrenia. Simple schizophrenia is characterized by withdrawal to an inner world. Hebephrenic schizophrenia involves confused thought and speech. Paranoid schizophrenics have delusions and hallucinations, especially auditory ones. Catatonic schizophrenia involves disordered muscular activity, with movements being stilted or at the wrong speed, and often leads to an alteration between stupor and excitement. There is no unanimous view of the causes of schizophrenia. Some studies[2] have been taken as showing that heredity plays the key role, while other theories lay main emphasis on environmental factors.

1 Quoted by Arieti, *op. cit.*
2 E.g. Kallmann, *The Genetics of Schizophrenia,* 1938.

This cursory summary of psychiatric classification of neuroses and psychoses gives only one of many classificatory systems. If one compares textbooks of psychiatry with textbooks of chemistry, one is struck by the anarchic state of psychiatric thought, with arguments still raging over the validity of the most fundamental distinctions. Are the distinctions between neurosis and psychosis, or between organic and functional disorders, useful? Is there an illness called 'schizophrenia'? If so, does it include all 'paranoid psychoses'? These conceptual difficulties partly arise from and partly contribute to our ignorance of the causes of mental disorders. If we knew their causes, we could classify them on this basis. And at present our system of classi-fication hampers research. As some research workers have recognized, if 'schizophrenia' turns out to be a cluster of largely unrelated diseases, research into its genetic basis is unlikely to succeed. We are still at the stage of trying to classify mental dis-orders by clusters of symptoms. Even where we can remove some of the symptoms, as we sometimes can by using drugs, we often cannot explain our success.

Professor Eysenck has claimed[1] that there is very little correla-tion between diagnoses made of the same patients by different psychiatrists. The need for a better system of classification has led him to propose that, when dealing with what he calls 'behavioural' disorders (which he contrasts with 'medical' ones), the notion of 'disease' should be abandoned. He says it should be replaced by measurements of patients' positions on various 'dimensions of personality', which he claims can be objectively quantified.[2] But this proposal leaves the essential conceptual problems unanswered. Eysenck is aware of the criticisms that can be made of any distinction between organic and functional disorders, and admits that it is an open question whether his 'behavioural' disorders will not one day be swallowed up by the 'medical' category, yet he maintains that his distinction has practical value at present. But, if it is possible that the behavioural disorders may one day be explained in terms of physical or chemical malfunctioning, it is less obvious that it is mistaken to think in

1   *The Scientific Study of Personality*, 1952; and in *The Effects of Psychotherapy*, in his *Handbook of Abnormal Psychology*, 1960.
2   'Classification and the Problem of Diagnosis', in H. J. Eysenck (ed.), *The Handbook of Abnormal Psychology*, 1960.

terms of 'disease'. And, if the behavioural disorders are not to be explained in physical or chemical terms, the problem remains of explaining why some patterns of behaviour should count, if not as diseases, at least as 'disorders'.

Whether one classifies certain types of mental states and behaviour in terms of the orthodox psychiatric apparatus of neuroses, psychoses and personality disorders, with their various subdivisions, or whether one uses classifications derived from Eysenck's tests, the central conceptual problem posed by the sceptics remains: what, if any, are the grounds for distinguishing between mental or behavioural disorder or illness on the one hand, and other abnormalities or mere eccentricity on the other?

4 MENTAL ILLNESS AND MORAL CHOICE[1]

It may be that increasing knowledge of the causes of mental illness will make us change our minds about whether or not someone's behaviour should be seen as symptomatic of illness. If we found that a certain type of delusion was caused by some chemical abnormality, we would be inclined to look again at our belief that someone was merely eccentric if his 'eccentricity' was caused by that same abnormality. We have been reminded by Professor Putnam[2] that only the discovery of the virus causing polio enabled us properly to distinguish between the symptoms of polio and similar manifestations resulting from other causes. We must accept that any purely behavioural distinction between mental illness and eccentricity will always be open to revision in the light of new knowledge of causal mechanisms. But, even if we had a complete causal understanding of all human behaviour, this would not in itself be a sufficient condition of our simply 'seeing' the difference between eccentricity and mental illness. For the distinction is in part (though *only* in part) a matter of moral choice.

1 I am grateful to Mr J. Melzack for his energetic and persuasive criticisms of an earlier draft of this section, and of parts of the next chapter. He should not be held responsible for what I say: I have sometimes accepted and sometimes resisted his arguments.
2 'Brains and Behaviour', in Butler (ed.), *Analytical Philosophy* (Second Series), 1965.

If someone is ill, whether physically or mentally, this is normally taken as a good reason for advising him to seek any satisfactory treatment that may be available. In exceptional circumstances, there may be good reasons for advising a person to reject a reliable cure. But cases where a large pension is brought in by a mild illness, whose cure is both painful and expensive, are not the norm. One does normally advise treatment for illness, but not for eccentricity. The question of whether or not to advise treatment is a moral question, and within limits there can be reasonable disagreement as to how it should be answered.

Those who take a very physiological view of mental illness may object here, in the light of a possible hypothesis about its causes. They may hold that, ultimately, all mental illness is to be explained in terms of some physiological or chemical malfunctioning. They may claim that, when we have enough knowledge of physiological or chemical mechanisms, all moral choice in this matter will be obliterated. To know whether or not someone is ill, we will only need look for the presence or absence of bodily malfunctioning.

But to say this is to take too naïve a view of bodily malfunctioning. What is it for something to be wrong with one's body?

It is possible when expressing scepticism about mental illness to make our knowledge of physical illness seem more clear-cut than it is. Our understanding of many bodily, as well as of many mental, disorders compares unfavourably with the standard set by our knowledge of phenylketonuria.[1] And the symptoms of physical disorders are sometimes hard to separate from the condition of many people who are not ill. To feel very tired and lethargic, or to have occasional headaches, can be symptoms of illness, or may have other more circumstantial causes. But the decision that someone is physically ill is not arbitrary. The evidence that someone is ill can be very strong or very weak, but the strength of this evidence can be rationally assessed. There are various kinds of evidence that we normally accept. The patient may complain that he is 'not himself', meaning perhaps that his feelings of weakness and lethargy have not been part of

---

[1] Sickle-cell anaemia is the disorder whose explanation is most complete and at the same time of greatest intellectual beauty. But at present we have no cure for it, while we can deal with disorders far less well understood.

his previous normal experience. Or he may find that his ability to perform certain tasks is diminished, as when he is unable to lift weights that would previously have caused him no difficulty, or when he can no longer read small print. Or, even in cases where the patient is unaware of any symptoms, medical examination may reveal something going wrong in his body, as when the early stages of cancer are detected.

With physical illness it is possible without too much difficulty to say why one counts some physical abnormalities as 'defects' or 'malfunctioning'. This is done by reference to the function of the part of the body in question, or to the effects of the physical abnormality on the body as a whole. Paralysis of a leg counts as something physically wrong because it prevents the leg from fulfilling its normal function in the movement of the body from place to place. The early stages of cancer count as something physically wrong because cancer prevents parts of the body performing their normal function and finally leads to pain and death. Where brain damage or some chemical abnormality causes amnesia, impaired intelligence or moods of deep depression, one can speak of 'malfunctioning' because the physical or chemical state is abnormal in a way that is harmful to the person who has it. But here one is already on the no doubt blurred border between physical and mental illness.

A number of statistically abnormal types of behaviour might be found to be in part caused by some unusual physiological or chemical state. It may be that people who have hallucinations all have some identifiable physiological peculiarity. But it may also be that those in our society who become fascists all have abnormal amounts of some chemical in their brain. Are we automatically to identify this as a 'malfunctioning' and thus classify them as mentally ill? Those who are not troubled by this example may be more disturbed by another: there might be some physiological or chemical peculiarity that had the effect of greatly improving a person's ability at mathematics, and had no other observable effect. Would this be a 'malfunctioning' that would force us to say that such a person needed treatment?

It is not mere physical and chemical abnormality that makes us say that someone is either physically or mentally ill, but the effects of the abnormality must also be taken into account. Some abnormalities may have effects that incline us to recommend treatment; some abnormalities may have effects we could reasonably wish to see preserved. And the question of which physical or chemical abnormalities, or which mental states or patterns of behaviour, we ought to see as justifying us in advising treatment is a moral question.

But this is not to concede the extreme sceptic's point that 'mental illness' is a wholly arbitrary classification of no scientific value. For the argument advanced here makes 'mental illness' no more 'arbitrary' than 'physical illness'. It is a matter of moral choice which physical conditions we see as needing treatment. One can imagine a society in which it was thought undesirable to be too energetic, and in which people who were not sufficiently lethargic were given treatment to damp down their energy. It is because there is a general consensus (no doubt for good reasons) as to which physical conditions ought if possible to be treated, that we overlook the element of moral choice here.

At present we do not have the same consensus over questions of mental illness that exists over questions of physical illness. So any attempt to give an account of the conditions that 'we' take as evidence of mental illness would run into difficulties. The psychiatrists quoted by Lady Wootton, who count unhappiness or lack of conformity as evidence of a need for treatment, clearly have different views from many other people. For this reason, argument is appropriate as to the kinds of condition we should consider to be mental illness. No attempt will be made here to draw a sharp boundary between physical and mental illness. To propose that we should count, say, delusions, as indicative of mental illness is not to deny that the illness in question may turn out to be some abnormality of brain chemistry, requiring drug treatment rather than psychotherapy.

5 MENTAL ILLNESS AS A KIND OF HARM

Squire Mytton lived near Shrewsbury in the early nineteenth century.[1] He drank eight bottles of port a day, and often had wet feet as a result of the thinness of both his shoes and his silk stockings. In snowy weather he would wear very little when out

1 This account is derived from Edith Sitwell, *English Eccentrics*, 1958.

shooting wild-fowl, and once he was seen naked as he ran over the ice after some ducks. He often took part in brawls and when drunk would fall off his horse. He deliberately sought accidents when out with horse and carriage, once galloping over a rabbit warren to see if his horse would fall. One day he rode into the dining room on a bear: when he applied his spurs to the bear, he was severely bitten. He spent more than half a million pounds in the last fifteen years of his life, much of it on hunting and drinking, or on items like his hundred and fifty-two pairs of trousers and breeches. One night he was coming back from the races and counting his money as his carriage went along, when he fell asleep and the wind blew away several thousand pounds. When he once had a hiccup, he said 'Damn this hiccup, but I'll frighten it away,' picked up a lighted candle and set fire to his nightshirt. The hiccup did go away, but the Squire was appallingly burnt. He died at thirty-eight in a debtors' prison.

Some of Squire Mytton's behaviour could be taken for mere eccentricity if considered in isolation. Peculiarities of dress, exaggerated enthusiasm for shooting or for drunken brawling are found among many whose sanity is not in doubt. But amusement at the Squire is quickly replaced by more mixed feelings as more of his behaviour is described. Laughter is not one's reaction to hearing of someone severely bitten by a bear, appallingly burnt or dying in a debtors' prison. The point where eccentricity shades into evidence of mental illness is the point where we start to pity a man, and, as in the case of Squire Mytton, pity begins where the odd behaviour is a sign of something harmful to the person concerned. Writing of his riding accidents, Dame Edith Sitwell says, 'John Mytton was as dangerous to others as to himself'. If his style of riding were not dangerous, one might regard it as merely eccentric; because it carried with it a very strong possibility of harm to himself, we are inclined to see it as a symptom of mental disorder. Riding on a safely muzzled bear is eccentric; those who ride unmuzzled bears usually need a psychiatrist.

The proposal I wish to make is that we should only regard someone as ill, and hence in need of treatment, where he is in a physical or mental condition that is harmful to him. (I use this phrase 'physical or mental condition' in a way that does not presuppose that these are distinct.) The condition may be harmful because it involves impairment of abilities, or for some other reasons to be discussed in the next section. Some conditions that satisfy this requirement are already clearly identified as physical illnesses, and these need not detain us. What is important here is that this proposal sets limits to what can be treated as mental illness. The insistence that mental illness must be harmful to the ill person, rather than characterizing it as a kind of 'deviance', is a necessary (but not a sufficient) defence against some of the evils pointed to by Lady Wootton and other critics of psychiatric diagnosis. Perhaps there are good reasons why the community, in its own interests, should use manipulative techniques to change someone's beliefs, attitudes or behaviour. But let us at least be clear that we are doing this in our own interests as a community, and not slur this over with misleading talk of curing an illness.

To avoid misunderstanding, it must be stressed that this proposal does not entail that all conditions of a person that are harmful to him should be treated as illness. It merely excludes the possibility of other conditions being so treated. But it is a suggestion that needs elucidation.

I have argued that the key feature of the mental condition of someone whom we should treat as mentally ill is not 'deviance' or 'abnormality', but harmfulness. It is a necessary, but not a sufficient, condition of a person's being mentally ill that his condition is harmful to himself. This proposal needs further elaboration, partly because it is necessary to say which kinds of harm are relevant to mental illness, and partly because of the obscurity of the concept of 'harmful condition' itself. This second problem is more fundamental and will be discussed first.

6 THE CONCEPT OF A HARMFUL CONDITION

This concept is in some ways similar to Bentham's concept of 'pain'.[1] Bentham talks of pains in such a way as to include not merely physical pains, but also disagreeable states of mind, which may be induced either by something positively unpleasant or else merely by the absence of something desired. Bentham divides pains into twelve kinds, some of which he further subdivides.

1 *Principles of Morals and Legislation*, Ch. 5.

There are Pains of Privation, resulting from unsatisfied desires, disappointment, or regret, either for unrepeatable past pleasures, or for opportunities for pleasure that were lost. There are Pains of Sense, which include hunger and thirst, excessive heat or cold, pains caused by disease or by exertion, and unpleasant tastes, smells, tactile sensations, sounds, sights or visual images. Then there is a heterogeneous group of pains classified as Pains of Awkwardness (resulting from lack of skill), Pains of Enmity, Pains of an Ill-Name, and Pains of Piety ('the pains that accompany the belief of a man's being obnoxious to the displeasure of the Supreme Being: and in consequence to certain pains to be inflicted by his especial appointment, either in this life or in a life to come'). There are Pains of Benevolence and Malevolence, the former resulting from pains suffered by other people, and the latter resulting from pleasures enjoyed by one's enemies. Finally there are Pains of Memory, Imagination, Expectation and Association. Bentham distinguishes among these pains between those that are 'extra-regarding' and those that are 'self-regarding': some are responses to the pleasure or pain of others, while some are not.

There is a prima facie case for saying of a condition that it is harmful to someone whenever it is seen as unpleasant or unwanted by him, or whenever it deprives him of pleasure or of the satisfaction of his wants. The breadth of Bentham's account of 'pain' is a reminder of the variety of conditions other than simply physical pain that can be unpleasant or unwanted. Feelings of hunger, frustration, anxiety or humiliation can seem just as undesirable as pain. But there are some harmful conditions that are not 'pains', even in Bentham's extended sense of this term. In the early stages of cancer, one may be quite unaware of one's condition, and feel neither physical pain nor any kind of anxiety or frustration. And some of Bentham's pains would not normally be thought of as harmful to those who have them. I may feel regret when I hear of someone being tortured in a South African prison, but it would be curious for me as a result to claim that I am among those harmed by the South African situation. Bentham's 'extra-regarding pains' are not included in the category of harmful conditions.

Some states that are unpleasant or unwanted, or involve deprivation, are not thought harmful because they bring to the person who has them some adequately compensating benefit, or else because they lead to the avoidance of some greater harm. Thus a person is not harmed when deprived of the pleasure of smoking if this deprivation is a successful attempt to prevent him from developing lung cancer. But unpleasant or unwanted conditions, or states of deprivation, are always prima facie harmful: if it is to be claimed that they are not harmful, this must involve citing future unpleasant or unwanted conditions that they help to eliminate, or else future conditions that they help to bring about, the absence of which would be some kind of deprivation.

This account of harmful conditions has been 'want-regarding' rather than 'ideal-regarding'.[1] To be harmed is to be given what is unpleasant or unwanted (or to be deprived of what is pleasant or wanted) without compensating benefit; it is not to be deprived of what others think is 'good for one' or to be given what they think is 'bad for one'. Thus you may disapprove of my drinking or gambling, but your view that one is a better sort of person if one does not drink or gamble is not sufficient to show that I am harmed by these habits. To establish this, you would have to show that drinking, gambling or their consequences involve reductions in my pleasure or want-satisfaction.

The main problems for this view of harm arise in cases of claims about unconscious deprivation. This can be illustrated by the case of homosexuality. It is often said that acts harmless to other people should not be legally forbidden. But can we be sure that homosexual acts do not harm others, perhaps by contributing to a social climate where people's homosexual tendencies are more readily developed? It is sometimes said that homosexuality is a condition that is harmful to the homosexual himself. Is homosexuality a 'personality disorder' calling for treatment, or is it an alternative way of life, seen as a disease only by the prejudiced? Someone might be harmed by his homosexual condition, solely because social prejudice created a furtive atmosphere around his relationships. But it might, on the other hand, be claimed that homosexuality would in itself be harmful to a person, even where it had full social approval. The truth or falsity of this claim could not be established by any simple test.

The mere fact that a homosexual would not wish to change is not enough to show that he is as well off as he would be if he were heterosexual. There are unconscious deprivations. A primi-

1 These terms are taken from Barry, *op. cit.,* Ch. 3.

tive tribesman may be contented, and able to satisfy his few wants, and yet suffer real deprivations. Even if he would not change, his sons, having experienced both tribal life and a more 'advanced' education and type of life, may have no wish to return to the simpler life. People who have developed a wider range of interests and desires rarely regret this in itself. (Addicts are among the exceptions.) Where those with experience of two ways of life are normally decisive in their preference for one, we have strong evidence that the other involves real deprivation.[1] An obvious reason for being reluctant confidently to ascribe unconscious deprivations to a contented homosexual is the absence of a sizeable group reporting their preferences after experiencing homosexuality and heterosexuality as ways of life.

People often go to psychiatrists because they are made miserable by their compulsive habits or by their moods of depression. Here there is no doubt that they are harmed. But if someone is in the state of inertia and withdrawal said to be typical of simple schizophrenia, it may be harder to show that this state is harmful to him. It may not be clear that he finds it unpleasant, nor that his abilities are in any way impaired. There may be many activities he has given up, but this is not in itself proof of inability.

In deciding what constitutes harm, it is easy to include too little or too much. It is tempting to think that I must always be the final authority on whether or not I am harmed by something. But this is false: for years many people were harmed by smoking without realizing it. And many people are unaware of the deprivations they suffer on account of the narrow limits of their education or of the community in which they live. But this is not to support the extreme alternative view, by which one assumes that men must be unconsciously harmed or deprived whenever they have a form of life that one would not oneself choose. It is perhaps out of this reaction against the first view that comes arrogant talk of forcing men to be free. Some limits must be set to the legitimacy of saying that a man is unconsciously harmed or deprived.

1 Only strong evidence, not conclusive proof. For scepticism about this kind of evidence, cf. Dr Steven Lukes, 'Alienation and Anomie', in Laslett and Runciman (eds.), *Philosophy, Politics and Society* (Third Series), 1967. This sort of evidence is that favoured by Mill for deciding questions of this kind, but he seems not to have fully appreciated the difficulties of it. Cf. *Utilitarianism*, Ch. 2.

In the case of someone in a state of prolonged withdrawal, but with no other symptoms, we can only say that his condition is harmful to him if he seems distressed himself, or else if we have strong evidence of unconscious deprivation. The best evidence can only be provided by those who have experienced both normal life and the state of withdrawal. Since people in the withdrawn state are normally unwilling to discuss it, we must turn to those who have experienced it and then been cured. It is only because they say they are glad of the change that we have any right to describe it as a 'cure'. It may be objected here that being a grateful ex-patient is not proof that one has been ill. One remembers the brainwashing in Orwell's *1984*, which was only complete when the critic saw his previous beliefs as mental illness and felt grateful for being cured.[1] But this brainwashing differs from the psychiatric treatment of schizophrenia just in that gratitude is deliberately induced by non-rational manipulative techniques. That such techniques are needed, to induce the belief that one has been mentally ill, is in itself evidence that this final belief is a delusion.

7 WHAT KINDS OF HARMFUL CONDITION QUALIFY AS MENTAL ILLNESS?

The view that one should treat as illness only those bodily or mental conditions that harm the person who has them leaves open the question of which among such states should be so treated. This question could only be satisfactorily answered in the context of the wider issue of the morally desirable limits of paternalism. But there are some plausible guiding principles. The condition must be 'directly' harmful: the harm must result from my mental or physical state itself, without the reactions of other people to my state being a necessary condition of the harm. A man's taste for chewing garlic may harm him by alienating his friends, but this hardly makes it a form of mental illness. And the same holds for unpopular political opinions, which in the same way may be 'indirectly' harmful. Physical or mental suffering are harmful in themselves, even if they have no further harmful

1 Mr J. E. Havard reminded me of this example. I have benefited from conversations on this point both with him and with Mr R. Kraty.

consequences. Impaired abilities are harmful because they reduce pleasure and want satisfaction, and because they can be distressing in themselves.

A second guiding principle concerns degree and duration. Just as some disagreeable physical conditions are too trivial or too transitory to be counted as physical illness, so a day or so of mild depression on failing an examination seems too insignificant to call for treatment as a mental illness. And, conversely, the more severe or prolonged the harmful condition, the more case there is for treating it as illness. Recognition that mental illness is in this way a matter of degree, without a sharp boundary, may help undermine the myth that the mentally ill are somehow different in kind from the rest of us.

It has been argued here that mental illness is no more of a myth than physical illness. Those who are sceptical about this concept are often alarmed by the authoritarian potentialities of psychiatry as a social institution.[1] They fear that the scope of the obscurely defined 'mental illness' may expand until psychiatrists have dangerous power over us all. And so I make two disclaimers. To argue that mental illness is not a myth is not to argue for increasing the power of psychiatrists. It is not suggested that psychiatrists should have the right to detain the mentally ill any more than doctors should have the right to detain the physically ill. In extreme cases there may be a paternalist case for such detention, but this needs separate argument. And where a mentally ill person is dangerous to others, there will be a case for detaining him, but this is on account of the danger rather than the illness itself. And the second disclaimer is that defence of the concept of mental illness is not a defence of authoritarian methods within psychiatric institutions. One need not be sceptical about the concept to believe that a libertarian approach is often likely to be more effective, as well as more decent, than other methods of treatment.

1   Cf. Szasz, *Law, Liberty and Psychiatry*, 1963.

7

MENTAL ILLNESS
AND IMPAIRED ABILITIES

I think that, although the present law lays down such a definition of madness, that nobody is hardly ever really mad enough to be within it, yet it is a logical and good definition.

Lord Bramwell, in 1874. (Quoted in the *Report of the Royal Commission on Capital Punishment,* 1953)

The erratic history of the English law's attempts to deal with the problem of the responsibility of the mentally ill has often been outlined.[1] Rules stating when mental disorder can reduce or abolish someone's legal responsibility for a crime seem always to have been either too narrow or too vague. Notoriously, the M'Naghten Rules were too narrow. The key passage states that 'to establish a defence on the ground of insanity, it must be clearly proved that, at the time of the committing of the act, the party accused was labouring under such a defect of reason, from disease of the mind, as not to know the nature and quality of the act he was doing; or if he did know it, that he did not know that he was doing what was wrong'. It is a familiar and crucial objection to these rules that one's capacities can be impaired without this leading to ignorance of what one is doing, or to the 'psychopathic' symptom of not understanding what is wrong.

1 By far the best account known to me of this history is that of Dr Nigel Walker, in his *Crime and Insanity in England,* Vol. I, 1968.

The impaired capacities of an alcoholic are a case in point.[1]

The search for more generous categories of exemption has led to a number of rules and proposals that make the grounds of exemption either too broad or too vague. At the other extreme from the M'Naghten Rules is the rule laid down in 1954 in the famous Durham case. The ruling of the United States Circuit Court of Appeals was that 'an accused is not criminally responsible if his unlawful act was the product of mental disease or mental defect'. This rule is open to obvious objections. How great a causal role must mental disease play for an unlawful act to be its 'product'? Why should all acts caused by mental illness go unpunished? Normally we think mental illness relevant to responsibility because it involves impaired capacities, but the Durham Rule by-passes all questions of capacity. In doing so, it omits a crucial stage of the argument needed to justify waiving punishment that would normally be administered.

Other attempts to replace the M'Naghten Rules have sometimes recognized that impairment of capacities is the crucially relevant feature of mental illness, but have often stated this in terms too general to be of much help. The American Law Institute's Model Penal Code says, 'A person is not responsible for criminal conduct if at the time of such conduct as a result of mental disease or defect he lacks substantial capacity either to appreciate the criminality (wrongfulness) of his conduct, or to conform his conduct to the requirement of law.' It adds that 'The terms "mental disease or defect" do not include an abnormality manifested only by repeated criminal or otherwise anti-social conduct.' A similar approach is adopted by the German Criminal Code, under which the relevant question is whether the accused 'lacked the ability to recognize the wrongness of his conduct and to act in accordance with that recognition'. The weakness of these admirable statements of the types of impaired capacity that are relevant, is that they give no guidance as to how one is to decide whether or not a particular person's capacities are impaired in the relevant respects.

In English law, the plea of 'diminished responsibility' was

[1] For histories drawn from legal cases where mental disorders have involved impaired capacities not covered by the M'Naghten Rules, cf. Biggs, *The Guilty Mind, Psychiatry and the Law of Homicide*, 1955, and especially Walker, *op. cit.*, where other inadequacies of the Rules are also discussed.

allowed in the 1957 Homicide Act. In section two of that Act, it was stated that 'where a person kills or is a party to the killing of another, he shall not be convicted of murder if he was suffering from such abnormality of mind (whether arising from a condition of arrested or retarded development of mind or any inherent causes or induced by disease or injury) as substantially impaired his mental responsibility for his acts and omissions in doing or being a party to the killing'. One may assume that the curious term 'his mental responsibility' was intended to refer to the mental capacities of the accused. The doctrine of this part of the Act can then be seen as an advance on the M'Naghten Rules, in that impairments of capacities other than those affecting reasoning or knowledge are recognized, but the Act gives as little detailed guidance as the Model Penal Code or the German Criminal Code.

As well as the 'special defences', which aim at modifying the court's verdict, there are the 'disposal procedures', under which the court, in deciding how to deal with a convicted offender, may take account of his mental disorder.[1] Under section sixty of the 1959 Mental Health Act, a court may in some circumstances order the detention of a convicted offender in a hospital. As well as other conditions being satisfied, a court must, on the evidence of the two medical practitioners, be satisfied 'that the offender is suffering from mental illness, psychopathic disorder, subnormality or severe subnormality'. It is sometimes suggested that the Mental Health Act gives us a model that we might use more widely. The traditional method of standing psychiatrists in the witness box to testify before the jury as to the mental health of a defendant has been found in many ways unsatisfactory. Dr Nigel Walker has described trials involving such testimony as 'a sort of game in which the psychiatrist in the witness box is like a wrestler who is compelled to box'. The disposal procedures are often seen as a potential replacement of the special defences, and as a means of avoiding the situation where a jury decides the result of a court-room contest between psychiatrists.

It is not the job of a philosophical book to make detailed suggestions about legal procedure. (Although decisions of legal procedure concerning when to consider medical evidence about

1 Cf. Dr Nigel Walker, 'Liberty, Liability, Culpability; *Medicine, Science add the Law*', 1965; reprinted in Craft (ed.), *Psychopathic Disorders*, 1966.

responsibility should be taken in the light of certain general considerations about law and punishment, some of which will be discussed in the next chapter.) But, for whatever reasons psychiatric testimony is considered, and whether before or after conviction, there are conceptual problems about mental illness and impaired abilities that must be answered before we can know what weight to give that testimony.

We have seen that there is sometimes scepticism about the whole concept of mental illness. The previous chapter contained an attempt to meet this scepticism, by suggesting that mental illnesses were a particular group of harmful conditions. But among these, some conditions were held to be harmful because they involved impaired abilities. Conditions involving delusions came into this category. But the concept of 'delusion' raises further difficulties, some of which have been cited by Dr R. D. Laing and others in support of their more general scepticism about mental illness. Do we not all have some false beliefs? When we say that someone is deluded, what more do we mean than just that he sees things differently from ourselves? In this chapter, a discussion of delusions will lead on to a more general discussion of impaired abilities involved in mental illness, and of their relevance to legal responsibility.

1 DELUSIONS AND THE IMPAIRMENT OF ABILITIES

If someone is said to have hallucinations, this need be no mere expression of his psychiatrist's prejudices. Here, there are objective tests, just as there are for colour-blindness. Someone who has hallucinations sees differently from other people.[1] But we do not, except when taking seriously the more neurotic philosophical doubts, wonder whether such a person sees things that are really there, but to which the rest of us are by some misfortune blind. This is because we can have such good evidence that this is not so. If someone thinks he is having a conversation with President Kennedy, all the other people round him can see that no one is there talking to him. And if some determined person says that all the observers may be wrong, there is all the

1 Or else he hears, feels, smells or tastes differently in parallel ways.

evidence that can be produced to show that President Kennedy died in 1963. Just as a colour-blind person does not have an equally adequate alternative way of seeing, but is unable to make discriminations that other people can make, so a man who has hallucinations is unable to make discriminations that are open to the rest of us. A schizophrenic with auditory hallucinations may be unable to discriminate in the normal way between a situation where someone is shouting abusively and one where all is calm and quiet.

Not all hallucinations are of the same type, and hallucinations in different contexts may influence one's powers of discrimination in different ways. If the hallucination is a symptom of schizophrenia, one may be quite unaware that reality does not correspond to one's experiences. But if the hallucination is the result of deliberately taking a drug, one may very well expect it to occur. Talking of his experiments with mescalin, sometimes taken by himself and sometimes taken by other people, Dr J. R. Smythies[1] says

> Some two hours after taking mescalin the subject will begin to see, if he keeps his eyes closed, vague patches of colour floating about in his visual field. These soon develop into more complex sensa: mosaics, networks, flowing arabesques, interlaced spirals, wonderful tapestries, and patterns and designs of all sorts, all swiftly coming and going and all in the most beautiful colours and exquisite design. Then formed objects appear, great butterflies gently moving their wings, fields of glittering jewels, silver birds flying through silver forests, golden fountains and golden rain, masks, statues, fabulous animals, soaring architecture, gardens, cities, and finally human figures and fully formed scenes where coherent histories are enacted. If the subject opens his eyes the colours of objects become much more intense, deep, rich, and glowing, and they change their shape in curious and pleasing ways.

It should be noted that in this account the experiences that bear no relation to reality only occur when the eyes are closed; when the subject opens his eyes his experiences are rather different. Smythies emphasizes this by saying that hallucinations brought on by mescalin

1 *Analysis of Perception,* 1956, p. 86.

do not occur as 'wild' sense-data integrated into an otherwise normal visual field. They are seen mainly with the eyes shut and are not integrated with the ordinary visual field at all, but are quite apart from it. When the eyes are open they usually disappear or form a faint background to the veridical visual field.

Where one knows that one has taken a drug that is hallucinatory, or where the hallucination occurs when one's eyes are shut, there may be little difficulty in discriminating between what is real and what is not. But in these cases there is no difficulty about objective tests for hallucination, for the very fact that a man has taken the hallucinatory drug, or has these experiences with his eyes shut, combined with the discrepancy between his report of his experiences and what others see, will count as good evidence that what he claims to see is not really there.

Some of the experiences described by patients as 'hallucinations' would be more correctly classified as 'illusions' than 'delusions'. Austin[1] says that the term 'illusion' in a perceptual context 'does not suggest that something totally unreal is conjured up', whereas 'the term "delusion" does suggest something totally unreal, not really there at all'. He goes on to say that the convictions of a man who has delusions of persecution can be completely without foundation, and says, 'For this reason delusions are a much more serious matter—something is really wrong, and what's more, wrong with the person who has them.' Austin's distinction between delusions and illusions corresponds closely to a distinction between two kinds of experience that can be had during schizophrenia. The anonymous author of 'An Autobiography of a Schizophrenic Experience'[2] says at one point,

> These visions could be divided into two categories. The first type had no relation to and was not suggested by surrounding objects in the material environment, but were entirely projections of inner states of consciousness and appeared before my eyes in the same way that a motion picture is presented to the eye of the observer. The second type did not constitute true visions, but could rather be called visual hallucinations and distortions, sometimes suggested by the

[1] *Sense and Sensibilia*, 1962, pp. 23–24.
[2] *Journal of Abnormal and Social Psychology*, 1955.

play of light and shadow, etc., acting upon an overwrought imagination. The true visions had definite but rather complex content and my attention was focused on grasping their meaning.

The experiences that were suggested by the play of light and shadow correspond closely to Austin's 'illusions' and in doing so undermine his implied assumption that only delusions, and never illusions, are symptoms of something wrong with the person who has them.

Where someone has illusions of this kind, as a result of some abnormal mental condition, it is again possible to say that this constitutes an impairment of a mental ability that can be objectively detected. Where it is possible for a person who has an illusion to detect the distortion, we can still speak of his powers of sensory discrimination being impaired, for an ability can be impaired without being altogether abolished. In this case the ability is impaired because an extra effort is needed in order to distinguish between the real and the merely apparent features of the environment. And where the person cannot even by making a special effort make this discrimination, he is in the same situation as someone who suffers from delusive hallucinations.

When one turns from hallucinations to other kinds of delusion, it seems harder to distinguish between those who are deluded and those who are not. It is here that Laing's case seems most powerful. Laing mentions the man who prefers to be 'dead rather than red', the man who says that negroes are an inferior race, and the world statesmen who boast of their nuclear weapons, and wonders how we distinguish between such people and those we say are suffering from delusions. It is quite true that many people have stupid or false beliefs that are not taken to be evidence of mental illness, but it can be argued that delusions are a special category of false beliefs.

Perhaps everyone, and certainly almost everyone, holds a number of false beliefs. It may be that all the evidence available at a given time supports an opinion that turns out to be false. Or one may hold beliefs that are not supported by evidence or which even go against the available evidence, perhaps because many other people hold those beliefs, or because one was brought up to hold them, or merely because they conform to one's prejudices.

One may accept the view of someone who has inadequate grounds for his belief, or one may oneself misinterpret the extent to which evidence or argument supports one's opinion. These are all familiar ways of falling into error, but they do not seem sufficient explanations of anything we would call a delusion. Those delusions that do not involve hallucinations may be beliefs that one is being persecuted, or that one is an insect, or that one has the atomic bomb inside one. Beliefs of this kind are not to be assimilated to the belief that negroes are an inferior race, if only because ignorant prejudices about negroes are quite common, and in order to be retained require only a determination not to look into the facts. But a false belief that one is an insect is not an opinion that might easily be absorbed from other people, and here the discrepancy is one between one's belief and evidence that can hardly be avoided.

It is important to distinguish between false beliefs that can be explained mainly in social terms and false beliefs that must be explained mainly in personal terms. At first glance a belief in the international communist conspiracy held by an American senator may seem essentially similar to an individual mental patient's delusions of persecution. But the difference is that the senator's belief can be explained in terms of the prevailing ideology in America. Many people share his belief, which is supported by widespread publicity, and in some circles social disapproval is attached to those who dissent from it. Although there exists no generally agreed causal explanation of the growth and persistence either of ideologies in general or in particular of the ideology of which this belief forms a part, it is surely clear that the senator's view is unlikely usefully to be explained by postulating that he is mentally ill. It will best be explained by providing a general account of why the beliefs that are common throughout a whole society are as they are. Historians do not find talk of 'delusions' helpful in explaining why most Europeans once believed in witchcraft, and anthropologists would not increase their understanding of primitive religion by regarding a tribe's beliefs as symptoms of a collective insanity. There seems no reason to consider believers in the international communist conspiracy any more deluded than believers in witchcraft.

An individual who has delusions of persecution is not merely a man who holds a false belief. He is someone whose false belief cannot be explained except in terms of some personal incapacity. If the system of beliefs prevalent in his society included the view that systematic persecution of a man by a hostile group was very common, we would change our attitude towards this view. Instead of seeing it as the kind of delusion that is symptomatic of mental illness, we would be likely merely to regard it as a socially conditioned false belief. But false beliefs are not all either the result of a society's ideology or else delusions. If a man falsely thinks he is attractive to women, or that his I.Q. is higher than it is, we do not regard this as a delusion. It may be objected that we do commonly talk of people being deluded about their attractiveness or their intelligence, but this is merely a colloquial use. Someone who exaggerates his intelligence is not normally deluded in the same sense as someone who thinks he is an insect. The crucial difference is that people who over-estimate their abilities are in most cases open to rational persuasion, however hard at times this may be. A man who falsely thinks that his I.Q. is well above average will normally modify his view when presented with a fair number of his intelligence tests results. A man who falsely thinks he is an insect is presumably not open to rational persuasion, since he is permanently confronted with overwhelming evidence against his belief.

It is not the content of a false belief that makes it the kind of delusion that is evidence of mental illness. It is rather the extent to which the belief is adhered to despite the evidence against it. The man who over-estimates his I.Q. is in the same category as the man who thinks he is an insect, if a sufficiently large quantity of evidence as to his lower I.Q. does not shake his belief. In such cases we conclude that we are in the presence of someone who is unable in this respect to respond to rational persuasion. And where we can find no cause for this inability in the belief systems of the society or in social pressures, we can only explain it by postulating something wrong with the person in question.

What is there in common between the different kinds of delusion that we regard as psychiatric symptoms? The answer suggested here is that they can all be regarded as showing abnormal impairment of some mental ability. Hallucinations, because they involve being deceived by the senses, can be seen as showing an impaired ability to discriminate between what is and what is not going on around one. And perceptual illusions that can by an effort be corrected are signs of a similar, if less serious, impairment, for no special efforts are needed when one's powers are unimpaired. Those false beliefs that do not involve sensory deception, but which yet count as delusions in the psychiatric sense, can equally be regarded as being a product of abnormally impaired abilities. Where I hold a false belief despite being presented with overwhelming evidence against it, and my doing so cannot be explained in terms of the beliefs common in my group or society, the only explanation that seems to be left is that my reasoning abilities are impaired to an abnormal extent.

2 MENTAL ILLNESS AND RESPONSIBILITY

Some mental illness causes harm, perhaps in the form of suffering, without impairing the person's abilities. This may be sufficient to count as mitigation or excuse, depending on the degree of the wrong committed and on the extent to which the harm makes the right course of action disadvantageous to the agent. But here there is nothing special about mental illness: the situation would be the same if the suffering were caused by migraine or by a slipped disc. It is only in cases where the mental illness involves impaired abilities that special problems about responsibility arise. It is said that kleptomaniacs cannot control their stealing, that alcoholics cannot control their drinking, that neurotics cannot control their ritual behaviour, or that psychopaths cannot control their anti-social acts. Here, the type of plea that is relevant is one of 'unalterable intention', discussed in Chapter 5 in the context of alcoholism.

In a legal system that recognizes a plea of this kind as either removing or reducing someone's responsibility, psychiatrists may be asked in a particular case whether such a plea can be substantiated. Those who examine the precarious foundations of psychiatric classification of mental illness find it tempting to react against attaching any weight to psychiatric testimony, on the grounds that too little is known, even of how to classify symptoms, to support judgments of capacity based on diagnoses now possible.

In ordinary life we often, with varying degrees of confidence, judge that someone's mental capacities are impaired. Compulsive rituals and neurotic fears are often noticeable. The incapacities of a psychopath may be harder to detect, but a perceptive person might come to realize that someone he knew had psychopathic traits, both from his actions and from conversations. It is not clear that a psychiatrist has any special insight which enables him to detect the limitations of a person's capacities. Often he must have to base his judgment on evidence available to any discerning person willing to ask questions. No doubt sometimes he knows from psychiatric experience or textbooks that particular impairments are often correlated with various other states, but only in such cases is he especially qualified to provide the answers.[1]

This is not an argument against attaching value to psychiatric evidence in a legal system where questions of responsibility are raised. The atmosphere of courts may often not be conducive to investigation of a person's mental capacities, and in such investigations psychiatrists have the advantage of being detached from the whole legal process. And, because of the knowledge they do have, it is preferable that psychiatrists, rather than other kinds of social worker, should be called upon. But it is crucial that psychiatrists should be asked the right question, rather than be posed some vague problem about whether the person is 'suffering' from 'diminished responsibility'. When it is recognized that the relevant plea is that of 'unalterable intention', one can see that the question the psychiatrist should answer is whether or not reasons providing a fairly strong motive for doing so would have persuaded the person to change his course of action. This is at least a clear question. Admittedly, openness to persuasion is a matter of degree, and also it will be often difficult to assess the extent to which someone is open to persuasion. Also the strength of the motive assumed for this hypothetical test will have to vary in order to be always stronger than the motive to commit the crime in question. But the fact that a question is hard to answer does not show that it is not the relevant one to ask. And the fact

1 There is a typically difficult problem raised by the question of the responsibility of men born with an extra Y chromosome. At present we do not know enough about them to decide whether their condition always, usually, or even often, involves impairment of abilities. At present we can only guess about this on the basis of evidence that suggests that the condition is highly correlated with certain types of crime. Cf. Jacobs *et al.*, *Nature*, 1965; Casey *et al.*, *Nature*, 1966; Price and Whatmore, *British Medical Journal*, 1967; Bartlett *et al.*, *Nature*, 1968.

that 'unalterable intention' is a matter of degree does not show that it is not still a good excuse.[1] The other excuses we recognize present similar problems. We have seen that whether or not a movement is involuntary may be a matter of degree; there is no sharp boundary between those unintentional acts that we excuse and those we consider negligent; there is only a blurred line between circumstances that excuse intentional acts, and some of those that do not.

The way in which psychiatric knowledge is relevant to questions of capacity is brought out in the case of psychopathy. The 1959 Mental Health Act says that for its purposes

'psychopathic disorder' means a persistent disorder or disability of mind (whether or not including subnormality of intelligence) which results in abnormally aggressive or seriously irresponsible conduct on the part of the patient, and requires or is susceptible to medical treatment.

The American Psychiatric Association's official classification of mental disorders includes 'anti-social reaction' under the heading of 'Personality Disorders', together with others such as sleep-walking, enuresis, speech distrubance, drug addiction, alcoholism and sexual deviation. It has been said that the essential characteristic of psychopaths is 'an inability ever to resist the impulse or temptation of the moment'.[2] Another central feature is said to be lack of love or affection for others. There are other features of psychopathy, said to be derivative from these, such as aggressiveness, lack of shame, an inability to learn from experience, and 'a lack of drive or motivation'.[3]

'Psychopathy' is especially open to the charge of being a term like 'lumbago', which purports to be a diagnosis but is in fact only a name for the symptoms. It is sometimes said that to call

1 This involves a rejection of an argument used in the *Report of the Royal Commission on Capital Punishment*, 1953: 'For the present we must accept the view that there is no qualitative distinction, but only a quantitative one, between the normal average individual and the psychopath, and the law must therefore continue to regard the psychopath as criminally responsible.' (Para. 401.)
2 Neustatter, *Psychological Disorder and Crime*, 1953.
3 Craft, 'The Meanings of the term "Psychopath"', in Craft (ed.), *Psychopathic Disorders*, 1966.

someone a psychopath is merely to absolve him from responsibility for one crime on the highly dubious grounds that he has unrepentantly committed many others.[1] But some studies suggest that many psychopaths have abnormal electroencephalograph waves, showing a predominance of large, slow waves, like those of young children. It is also claimed that study of capillary loops in the nail bed shows that these are immaturely formed in a significantly larger proportion of psychopaths than of other people.[2] These studies suggest ways of identifying psychopaths independently of their behaviour.

We have seen that conscience can usefully be thought of, not simply in terms of the possession of information or the occurrence of guilt reactions, but also in terms of certain abilities. One independent means of identifying psychopaths is that they are notably lacking in just these abilities. Dr G. M. Stephenson[3] found that psychopaths have an unusually strong tendency to define wrong-doing in terms of law-breaking. Asked to list the worst things a person can do, psychopaths included shooting at beasts with air rifles, turning round one-way street notices, pulling gates off posts, and smashing bottles on the road. The replies of psychopaths were both unusually trivial and unusually specific. Psychopaths, unlike the control group, often seemed unable to give reasons for their views. It is hard to avoid the impression that these psychopaths are quite capable of mechanical obedience to rules, but have not developed moral capacities of reasoning and imagination.

If it is true that the cluster of traits and incapacities subsumed under 'psychopathy' is often found together, the knowledge that this is so will place a psychiatrist in a strong position to make inferences about incapacities from other evidence. Perhaps with future knowledge we will subdivide psychopaths into other more unitary categories. Then we may sometimes think our present judgments of capacity to have been mistaken. But the possibility of error is not a conclusive argument against letting psychiatrists use what knowledge they now have.

Some of the arguments of Chapter 6 throw doubt on the value of one plausible and attractive proposal. The difficulties of answer-

1 Cf. Wootton, *Social Science and Social Pathology*, 1959, pp. 249–251.
2 Stafford-Clark, *Psychiatry Today*, 2nd edition, 1963, p. 117.
3 *The Development of Conscience*, 1966.

ing questions about someone's capacities have led some of those who wish to preserve the links between capacities and liability to punishment to propose exemption by psychiatric category. Professor Hart says that 'instead of a close determination of such questions of capacity, the apparently coarser-grained technique of exempting persons from liability to punishment if they fall into certain recognized categories of mental disorder is likely to be increasingly used'.[1] He says that exemption by general category is an old technique in English law, being used to exempt all very young children from responsibility. Hart concludes that, despite certain difficulties he mentions, 'it seems likely that exemption by medical category rather than by individualized findings of absent or diminished capacity will be found more likely to lead in practice to satisfactory results'.

The difficulties Hart mentions are ones that require policy decisions to be taken within the machinery of legal exemption by medical category. There is the question of what should be done with an offender who, at the time of his trial, has either recovered from his disorder at the time of the crime, or has become mentally ill since his crime. Then there is the problem of whether or not a court should have to be satisfied that there was a causal link between the illness and the offence. And there are problems concerning whether psychiatric investigation should always or usually take place after, rather than before, the verdict of the court.

But the more fundamental difficulty suggested by a look at psychiatric categories is that they are themselves too obscurely delineated to be of much help. And even if, as is not the case, there were general agreement on how to classify patients, there would still be the problem of reaching agreement on the relationships between various illnesses and the impairment of various abilities. Because of our present ignorance and confusion, acceptance of Hart's proposal would lead to a strong possibility of people with unimpaired capacities being placed in categories exempting them from responsibility, and to the more disturbing possibility of those whose capacities are relevantly impaired being denied exemption on the basis of their diagnosis. If we

1 Postscript: 'Responsibility and Retribution', in *Punishment and Responsibility*, 1968. Cf. also 'Changing Conceptions of Responsibility', in *The Morality of the Criminal Law*, 1965, reprinted in *Punishment and Responsibility*.

were to exempt from responsibility, say, all schizophrenics, this would, in at least two ways, be unlike exempting all very young children. One is that, once we have decided on an age limit, there is no serious problem as to who counts as below that limit, while the difficulties of deciding who is to count as a schizophrenic are considerable. The second is that we have a great deal of knowledge as to the capacities of children (not that lack of capacity is the only reason for exempting them) while our knowledge of the capacities of schizophrenics is smaller.

The more flexible system of asking psychiatrists to make judgments of capacities allows them to use such knowledge as they have. One may also hope that knowledge will increase and that, as a result, categories of diagnosis will change. Since it is unlikely that changes in the law would always keep the list of exempting diagnoses up to date, Hart's proposal involves the danger of psychiatrists once again having to twist their evidence in order to force it into ancient medical categories insisted on by the law.

The system of exemption by medical category may be an improvement when there is agreement on clearly defined categories, as well as knowledge of the extent to which various disorders impair different abilities. Anyone who thinks that day has come is referred to the psychiatric textbooks.

8

PUNISHMENT

If an ox gore a man or a woman, that they die: then the ox shall be surely stoned. . . .

Exodus

A sow, mutilated and dressed in human clothing, was hanged at Falaise in 1386 for biting a child, and three years later a horse was hanged for killing a man at Dijon. In 1454 the Bishop of Lausanne initiated legal proceedings against the leeches which had infected the water at Berne. And in 1474 a cock was burned for having committed a crime against nature and laid an egg. Animals were often considered responsible for sexual offences committed upon them by human beings and were even tortured to elicit groans which were accepted as confessions . . . and as late as 1685 a bell was whipped 'to punish it for having assisted heretics'.

Christopher Hibbert: *The Roots of Evil*

Lord Hewart [*Lord Chief Justice in the 1920s*] suggested that the medical inquiry should be concerned only with a single, simple question: 'if this condemned person is now hanged, is there any reason to suppose from his state of mind that he will not understand why he is being hanged?'

Nigel Walker: *Crime and Insanity in England*

To some critics of present methods of dealing with those who break the law, the discussion of how best to determine someone's responsibility for his act seems unnecessary and unproductive. It is sometimes said that the whole conception of punishment is bound up with barbaric ideas of retribution, and should be replaced by a 'medical' approach, that sees crime as a kind of social disease, to be treated rather than avenged. And it is claimed that, within the context of this more enlightened attitude, questions of responsibility will not need to arise. Such claims must be attractive to any humane person who considers the past, and present, of the social institution of punishment. It is artificial to discuss questions of legal responsibility in isolation from questions about the purposes of legal punishment and the possibility of realizing them by other means.

All states have a penal system: an official mechanism designed to inflict suffering or deprivation on those who break the law. Many people take it for granted that such suffering is inevitable, and for them discussions of the justification of punishment are redundant. But others, while accepting the need for punishment, are led by their concern for its effectiveness to make explicit the aims they wish it to realize. Yet others are disturbed by any deliberate infliction of suffering, and demand that it should be justified before they will give it their approval. The problem has traditionally been considered mainly in terms of choosing between the rival claims of retributivists and utilitarians. It is said that a retributivist is one who considers that it is in itself desirable that wrongdoing should be followed by appropriate suffering. We are told that utilitarians, on the other hand, only support punishment where it is justified in terms of reforming the criminal or of deterring other potential criminals, to the extent of sometimes supporting the punishment of innocent people.

But the debate has gradually come to be conducted on a higher level of sophistication. It has been pointed out[1] that there are views that could be called 'retributivist' which are compatible with other views that could be called 'utilitarian'. One could support a retributivist account of the meaning of the word 'punishment', such that the infliction of suffering upon the innocent would not count as punishment. And this would be compatible with taking a utilitarian view of the problem of which

1   E.g. by Mr Anthony Quinton, 'On Punishment', *Analysis*, 1954; reprinted in Laslett (ed.), *Philosophy, Politics and Society* (1st series), 1956.

kinds of acts should be forbidden and thus punishable. But, as critics of such attempts at reconciliation have pointed out, there are many retributivists who hold the moral view that retribution is desirable for its own sake, instead of, or in addition to, holding the retributivist definition of punishment. And their view is still incompatible with utilitarianism. There is also the difficulty that some versions of the utilitarian doctrine do seem capable of justifying the infliction of suffering on the innocent, and, whether or not it is called 'punishment', this remains a serious objection to those doctrines.

The sophistication of the discussion has also been increased by distinguishing between various different moral questions to which retributivism and utilitarianism are among the rival answers. Professor Hart[1] has argued persuasively that

> different principles (each of which may in a sense be called
> a 'justification') are relevant at different points in any morally
> acceptable account of punishment. What we should look for
> are answers to a number of different questions such as:
> What justifies the general practice of punishment? To whom
> may punishment be applied? How severely may we punish?
> In dealing with these and other questions concerning
> punishment, we should bear in mind that in this, as in most
> other social institutions, the pursuit of one aim may be
> qualified by or provide an opportunity, not to be missed,
> for the pursuit of others.

Hart goes on to argue, in the context of the questions he singles out, that one can with consistency give a utilitarian justification of the general practice of punishment and at the same time support the principle of 'retribution in distribution': the principle that we may punish only an offender for an offence.

Along with an increasing awareness of the variety of questions that must be answered if any particular penal system is to be justified, there is an awareness of the variety of moral considerations that may be invoked in the answering of any one of

---

1 'Prologomenon to the Principles of Punishment', *Proceedings of the Aristotelian Society*, 1959–60. Reprinted as the first chapter of Hart, *Punishment and Responsibility*, 1968, cf. also Rawls, 'Two Concepts of Rules', *Philosophical Review*, 1955.

them.[1] It seems less and less helpful to discuss penal policy in terms of the crude categories of retributivism and utilitarianism. It is no doubt unprofitable to attempt to discuss, or even to list, all the possible reasons that could be advanced for punishing people. The pleasure given to sadists by the thought of criminals being punished is, after all, a possible reason for supporting various penal measures. But it is worth noting the variety of aims and principles to be found if one examines some of the main ones that could plausibly be advanced in a discussion of punishment among men both humane and rational. Adding one extra distinction to those mentioned by Hart, we can separate four central questions. What aims justify having the social institution of punishment? What methods of punishment should we use? How should we determine the amount of punishment appropriate in a given case? Whom should we punish?

1 PUNISHMENT AS A SOCIAL INSTITUTION

In considering the general justification for having the social institution of punishment, it is easy to assume perhaps too readily that an adequate justification can be found. Many in the anarchist tradition are unpersuaded that this is so: either on the grounds that social rules are alien to the good society, or on the grounds that rules need not be backed by penal sanctions. Those who dismiss this view as absurdly unrealistic should ask themselves what grounds they have for doing so.[2] And if the anarchists seem insufficiently hard-headed, we can turn to Bentham, and remember his insistence that there is a class of cases where punishment is needless because the purpose it serves can be equally well achieved by other means, at less cost in human suffering. Bentham's own example of this is any case where 'instruction' will be as effective as 'terror'. To ask for a justification of punishment need not be to presuppose that there is one.

One attempt to justify punishment consists in an appeal to

1   This pluralism is especially evident in an article by Professor Piamenatz, 'Punishment and Responsibility', in Laslett and Runciman, *Philosophy, Politics and Society* (3rd series), 1967.
2   Can human nature not be changed? How can one be sure?

retributive justice. On this view, it is fitting that those who have done what is forbidden should have the suffering they are said to deserve. It is argued that anything other than this would show a disregard for justice. Among objections urged against retributivism are that 'retribution' is a polite name for revenge, which is more generally recognized to be evil, and that retributivism exhorts us to cause suffering that benefits no one. But a determined retributivist may say either that revenge is not an evil, or else that retribution can be an impersonal affair without the feelings of hatred and pleasure that combine so unpleasantly in revenge. To the other objection he may simply reply that while retribution may benefit no one, it is not pointless since it is the only means of doing justice. The dispute over this matter seems to be one of the relatively rare cases where there is a clash between two moral views so basic that between them no argument seems possible. The retributivist can only wait in the hope that his opponent may in time have an intuition of the justice of retribution. His opponent can only point to the suffering that occurs in the name of retribution, and ask if it is really worth while.

Another reason sometimes advanced for having a penal system is that legal punishment provides a means whereby society can express its feelings of outrage at acts it finds particularly offensive. Durkheim (who was attempting an explanation rather than a justification) said that 'an act is criminal when if offends strong and defined states of the collective conscience'. And he went on later to say that 'Punishment consists, then, essentially in a passionate reaction of graduated intensity that society exercises through the medium of a body acting upon those of its members who have violated certain rules of conduct.'[1] Some who accept Durkheim's approach to punishment see the passionate reaction as consisting in retribution, and their view has already been noted. But others argue that it is right that we should punish offenders, not because retribution is desirable, but because, as Lord Denning put it, 'the ultimate justification of any punishment is not that it is a deterrent but that it is the emphatic denunciation by the community of a crime'.[2] This 'denunciatory' justification of a penal system is in need of elucidation. Is denunciation an end in itself, or is it a

1 *The Division of Labour in Society*, Ch. 2.
2 *Evidence to the Royal Commission on Capital Punishment*, 1953.

means to some further end, such as reducing the number of crimes committed? If the latter, it is not an alternative 'justification', but a view of the means by which one can best realize the utilitarian ends to be discussed below. But if denunciation is an end in itself, it appears either not to justify punishment, or else not to be distinguishable from retribution. For denunciation need not take the form of inflicting suffering on the offender.[1] If we wished to denounce a murder, we could arrange for the Archbishop of Canterbury or the Prime Minister to appear on television and on behalf of the community express feelings of outrage, instead of adding to human misery by sending the murderer to prison. But if it is insisted that the denunciation should take the form of the infliction of suffering, this seems to be merely the retributive theory in disguise.

The utilitarian argument in favour of a penal system is that it is an attempt to reduce the number of times the rules or laws of a society are broken. Here, punishment is thought of as having an effect either upon convicted criminals or upon potential ones. The punishment is intended to reform the criminal by making him see the error of his ways, or by making him afraid of the consequences of further crime. Or it is intended simply to prevent him, by locking him up, from breaking the law during the period of punishment. Or else it is thought that potential criminals will be persuaded of the wickedness of the offence or be made to fear the consequences of crime. These utilitarian aims are rarely criticized as being in themselves undesirable. Criticism normally takes the form either of saying that they are realized at too high a price, or else it comes from retributivists and others who say that these should neither be the only aims, nor the main ones, of a penal system.

Among other justifications sometimes advanced is the need to avoid the public taking the law into its own hands. It is suggested that if no system of punishment were institutionalized in a society, feelings of outrage at the breaking of rules would lead to lynch law. This unofficial retaliation is either regarded as evil in itself, or else as evil because the 'punishments' would be harsh or unjust, or else as evil because likely to lead to social disintegration. A parallel argument is sometimes brought forward, not to defend

1 As Mr S. I. Benn has pointed out, 'An Approach to the Problems of Punishment', *Philosophy*, 1958.

institutionalized punishment as such, but to defend the legal prohibition (and hence punishment) of particular kinds of action. The force of either of these arguments depends on the extent to which in a particular society the danger of such unofficial reprisals is a real one, and this is not a question to which there is an *a priori* solution.

Whether or not one supports the existence of the institution of punishment should depend on the extent to which one thinks that one or more of these aims is worth realizing, and upon the extent to which one thinks that such aim or aims can be realized without the sacrifice of other considerations one minds about more. On some moral views, the deliberate infliction of suffering is too high a price to pay for any benefit.

2   METHODS OF PUNISHMENT

It has sometimes been supposed that arguments in support of society's right to punish criminals are sufficient to justify whatever penal apparatus happens to be in existence at the time. But it is possible to approve of punishment without defending tortures, executions or even prisons. In considering arguments as to the rights and wrongs of particular methods of punishment, one need not dwell for long on the defence of various methods, for this will consist in claiming that they effectively realize one or more of the various general aims already discussed. Thus it may be claimed that heavy fines are an effective deterrent for some offences, or that capital punishment is an especially appropriate form of retribution for murder, since it 'fits the crime'. Or it may be said that probation has a better record of reforming criminals than some other penal methods.

But considerations not already touched upon can be invoked in criticism of techniques of punishment. One can appeal to the humanitarian principle that some punishments are too cruel to use, however effective they may be. This is perhaps the argument that most people would use against torture, and could without absurdity be invoked against capital punishment, corporal punishment or imprisonment. Notoriously, capital punishment is uniquely open to the objection that no redress is possible where a person punished turns out to have been innocent. Then there is the suggestion that some punishments are too degrading to the offender for their use to be permissible. This could be said of any of the punishments just mentioned, and is an objection that could be urged very strongly against any punishment that derives part of its force from the fact that it takes place in public. Some punishments, notably capital or corporal punishment, but perhaps also imprisonment, could be opposed on the grounds that they are bad for those whose job it is to administer them. (Would you wish your daughter to marry someone who made his living by hanging or flogging people?) There is also the objection that some punishments are harmful or degrading to people who neither suffer nor administer them. I can remember that, when I was aged about ten, children at the school I was at took great interest in executions, and would discuss them with subdued excitement, especially as the announced time of some particular execution drew near.[1] One needs little imagination to see the force of this as an objection to capital punishment.

Another insufficiently considered objection to some forms of punishment is that they bring suffering to people other than the offender. The life of a wife of a man in prison is likely to be one of loneliness, shortage of money, and sexual deprivation. She may be a victim of social stigma, and she is likely to be distressed by the suffering of her husband.[2] Wives are not the only relatives to suffer. One can imagine what it must be like to be the child of a man in prison, although we cannot yet calculate the long-term harm done to such a child. But perhaps capital punishment is most open to this objection: the period before an execution must be one of unspeakable suffering for the parents, wife or children of a condemned man.

Whether or not one supports a particular method of punishment should depend on the extent to which it realizes the penal aims one supports, on the extent to which it is open to objections one minds about, and on the extent to which other methods would either realize one's aims better or be less open to the objections. Some current penal methods may turn out both to be open

1 Miss Leila Berg, in her *Risinghill: Death of a Comprehensive School,* 1968, refers to 'such children as are white-faced the whole schoolday when a man is being hanged in the prison down the road' (p. 159).
2 Cf. the letter from a prisoner's wife in the *New Statesman,* 6 January 1967.

to many moral objections and to be ineffective when judged by their own aims.

3 THE AMOUNT OF PUNISHMENT

Justifications of inflicting a particular amount of punishment on someone normally appeal to the general aims of punishment. The familiar aims of retribution, denunciation, reform, deterrence and the others appear again. It is suggested that any less punishment would be insufficient retribution. Or it would be an inadequate denunciation, or not enough to reform him, or to deter others, or to protect him from unofficial retaliation. There is the additional principle, sometimes invoked, that like cases should be treated alike, so that if a man was given five years' prison last week for this very crime, it would be unjust to give this man only two years. This principle can equally be used to criticize a sentence as being too severe.

There are various principles that can be invoked to criticize the severity of a punishment.[1] It can be criticized on grounds of retributive justice, as being more than is deserved, either by the wickedness of the criminal's intention or by the harm done. Then there is the humanitarian principle that some amounts of punishment are too great to be given. Or there is the principle that some amounts of punishment are wrong because they cause too much suffering to the innocent family of the criminal. Then there is the utilitarian view that one should always use the minimum punishment needed to realize one's aims, and that the suffering caused by punishment should in no case exceed the suffering it prevents. It is also said that too great a punishment frustrates the aim of reforming the criminal.

It is sometimes suggested that retributive principles, whether used to set a maximum or a minimum limit to punishment, are especially open to the objection that there is no objective measure of retributive appropriateness.[2] But this objection seems to hold equally against any utilitarian rule intended to specify how much

1 The 30-year prison sentence passed on some of the 'train robbers' seems open to *all* the objections mentioned here.
2 Cf. Walker, 'The Aims of a Penal System', The James Seth Memorial Lecture, 1966. Anyone familiar with this lecture will realize that I have found it more helpful than my criticisms of it may suggest.

punishment is appropriate.[1] There are two different questions that must be answered in order to deal with this problem: there is the question of the relative amounts of punishment that should be given for different offences, and the question of the absolute amounts to be given. Thus, if we agree on the relative question, say that a man should be fined twice as much for his second conviction for tax evasion as for his first, there is still the question of how much he should be fined in either case. The retributivist has to answer these questions by invoking two intuitions. But the utilitarian also has to answer these questions. He must do this on the basis of judgments as to the amount of suffering caused by such crime, the amount caused by the punishment, and the extent to which the punishment will reduce the frequency of the crimes. It is only this last judgment that can in principle be made without any degree of arbitrariness. The powerful objections to retributivism are moral ones, and do not concern quantification. Difficulties about measurement are not unknown to utilitarianism.

4   AN APPROACH TO PUNISHMENT

The fourth question to be discussed ('whom should we punish?') is the one most closely related to the topic of responsibility. It is possible, before examining this last question, to outline an approach to punishment in the context of which to discuss questions of legal responsibility.

Traditional utilitarianism sought to resolve all moral questions into matters of whether or not certain acts or institutions were more likely than any possible others to bring about the goals of maximizing happiness and minimizing suffering. Criticisms of this doctrine are often practical ones. There are difficulties in measuring happiness, in comparing different kinds of happiness, in comparing the happiness of different people, and in predicting the consequences of one's actions. These practical difficulties are real, but they are perhaps not always as daunting as is sometimes thought. That happiness cannot be measured precisely does not seem a very formidable objection to the view that it would be increased if we produced and distributed enough food for every-

1   This point has been made by Mr C. W. K. Mundle, 'Punishment and Desert', *Philosophical Quarterly*, 1954.

one to have enough to eat. But there are other familiar criticisms of utilitarianism, of a more fundamental kind. These are moral criticisms, made from the standpoint of other values, such as justice, freedom, or the sanctity of life, that are held to have an importance that is independent of their contribution to human happiness.

The moral objections to utilitarianism may make one reluctant to say that the maximizing of happiness should be the only goal of social policy. But it is possible to outline a moral approach to punishment, retaining something of the spirit of utilitarianism, that is sufficiently different to meet many of these objections. The new doctrine would accept that to the appraisal within this moral approach of institutions or actions it is crucial whether or not, and to what extent, they benefit or harm people. (Though here, in order to allow room for moral objections to cruelty to animals, 'people' should perhaps be modified to 'conscious beings'.) But 'benefit' and 'harm' need to be interpreted more widely than the traditional utilitarian terms 'happiness' and 'suffering', or than the even narrower 'pleasure' and 'pain'. In a previous chapter[1] it was suggested that a harmful condition is one that reduces a person's pleasure or want satisfaction (whether or not he is aware of this) or one that increases his physical or mental suffering. And one can talk of a condition being harmful because it reduces someone's want satisfaction by comparison with what it might be, and not merely by comparison with what it was. The concept of harm in general is to be understood along these lines. Similarly, whether some act, policy or institution benefits someone depends on whether or not it increases his pleasure or want satisfaction, or else on whether or not it reduces his physical or mental suffering. On this view, pleasure is not the only benefit, nor pain the only harm. One can see that it could be argued that people benefit from having a large area of freedom, from having their individuality respected, or from an atmosphere of social equality. All of these, while arguably of intrinsic value in themselves, could be defended as means to the maximization of want satisfaction or pleasure, or to the avoidance of suffering. Similarly, distributive justice could, up to a point, be defended in these terms. When someone is given an unfairly small share of a benefit being distributed, he may be harmed by the frustration of

1 Chapter 6, section 6.

expectations or by the growth of resentment, over and above the harm which could be calculated merely by measuring the amount of the benefit lost.

I should not wish to defend the view that actions or policies should be judged solely in terms of human benefit or harm as outlined here. I do not wish to forgo the possibility of assigning to justice, freedom or other ends a value independent of their tendency to increase the balance of want satisfaction and pleasure over frustration and physical or mental suffering. But much of the attraction of traditional utilitarianism can be preserved by stipulating that an action or policy should be ruled out where it causes harm to anyone and yet no one benefits from it. This restriction does not rule out the pursuit of other ends, even where they do not increase the ratio of benefit over harm: all that is required is that as a result either someone benefits or else no one is harmed. It also leaves it open to us to introduce further restrictions limiting the kinds of benefit that are to count as acceptable justifications for causing harm: the pleasure a sadist gets from the suffering of another is one kind of benefit we may choose to exclude.

This restriction, that no one should be harmed where no one benefits, may seem completely trivial. It is certainly compatible with a variety of moral attitudes and beliefs. But it is not a wholly empty restriction. If, in pursuit of some ideal of social justice, we take from the rich and give to the poor, our restriction is not flouted, for the poor benefit. But if, unable to sell the millionaire's Rolls-Royce, we confiscate it and throw it into the sea, on the grounds that equality of deprivation is better than unfair luxury, we are flouting the restriction. We may not harm even the millionaire unless someone benefits from this. (I should wish to exclude the pleasure of others at hearing of the millionaire's loss from the category of justifying benefits, as I should wish to exclude a sadist's pleasure in the physical suffering of others.)

And, more relevant to the theory of punishment, there is the difficulty the restriction raises for the more aggressive forms of retributive justice. To demand that the guilty should suffer on purely retributive grounds would be to support a policy that created harm without compensating benefits.[1] Other people's

---

1 A person may benefit from being treated as a responsible agent. But it is hard to believe that treating someone as a responsible agent must sometimes involve inflicting retributive suffering on him.

pleasure at hearing of someone getting his deserts, a possible candidate for the role of a compensating benefit, could also be excluded from the category of acceptable justifications. But, in order to prevent an indefinitely long list of arbitrary exclusions of various kinds of benefit, it is necessary to reformulate the principle which should now be stated as follows: *An action or policy is always morally unjustifiable where it causes harm to anyone, and yet no one benefits from it in an acceptable way. A benefit is only unacceptable where it consists in pleasure of any kind at the misfortunes or suffering of others.* This principle rules out any attempt to justify punishing someone merely on the grounds that he deserves it. But it does not rule out the negative principle that people should not be given any punishment that they do not deserve. Nor does the principle say that *any* harm is justifiable provided that someone benefits from it.

What kinds of penal principles would be compatible with this restriction? There is no place for retribution as a general aim justifying the institution of punishment. The reduction of the crime rate is clearly a possible justifying aim, as is the avoidance of unofficial retaliation. But I should advocate subjecting these aims to two familiar utilitarian restrictions. One is that *we are only justified in punishing where there are good grounds for supposing that we are doing less harm than we are preventing.* This can only be the case where, as well as other conditions being satisfied, there is evidence that the abolition of punishment for a particular offence would significantly increase either the frequency of the 'crime' or else the probability of unofficial retaliation. And so it seems that serious acceptance of this approach to punishment would involve a willingness to experiment far more boldly than we do now. One relevant experiment would be to refrain from punishing a crime for a trial period to see how much difference to the crime rate this made. If total suspension of punishment for a crime was found to increase its frequency, there would then be room for a further experimental period in which punishment was administered, but in smaller doses. Only by means of such investigations can we be sure that we are not inflicting pointless suffering.

There is the further utilitarian restriction that *punishment is only justified where there are good grounds for thinking that, as a method of achieving the aims in question, punishment causes less harm than any other equally effective method.* Serious acceptance of this restriction would involve being ready to experiment with other methods, such as taking more seriously the possibilities of educating people to see the undesirability of various crimes. For this we could make use both of schools[1] and of the mass media. We could also change those features of the social environment that seem to stimulate crime.[2]

The view that punishment is a necessary feature of any practically possible human society seems needlessly dogmatic. There is no adequate evidence that human nature is so static that we cannot devise a society in which prohibitions backed by sanctions would be redundant. But it must be admitted, preferably grudgingly, that we do not now live in such a society. We are sufficiently willing to harm each other in pursuit of our own ends for restraining sanctions to be necessary. It is in this context that the aims of a penal system must be considered. In a system guided by the principles mentioned, the question of punishment only arises in restricted classes of cases. These are those where the most effective method of making someone give up crime is unpleasant, or at least unwanted by the offender, or where the offender is too dangerous to let loose, or where the punishment is aimed at deterring others. (For practical purposes in many communities one other type of case can be left on one side: that in which punishment might be administered to prevent unofficial retaliation.) And it is possible that increasing knowledge derived from experiments in doing without punishment, or in finding substitutes for it, will reduce the number of cases where punishment is permissible.

1 The contrast between the role of schools as it often is and as it might be is brought out in Miss Leila Berg's book on Risinghill.
2 Cf. Terence Morris, *The Criminal Area*, 1958. As means of reducing the amount of crime, education and changing the social environment are not the only alternatives to the use after the offence of punishment or treatment. 'Criminals' are not one homogeneous class. But there is evidence that many of the most anti-social among them have not been loved enough as children: often they have been 'unwanted' children. It seems that one method of reducing crime (and much other misery) would be by social expenditure on much more active and efficient education about contraceptives, and upon their free provision. Utilitarians also rightly point out that some acts are prohibited by law, but should not be. Here we could reduce the crime rate by repealing the laws.

5 MANIPULATION

A frequently voiced objection to penal policies with non-retributive aims is that they appear to involve manipulation of people. In the type of policy mentioned here, the danger of manipulation comes in at two points. There may seem a hint of Brave New World in the proposal to experiment in teaching children the undesirability of various crimes. And there is perhaps a sinister sound to the proposal that punishment should often be replaced by alternative methods of treatment.

The importance people attach to being treated as responsible agents underlies some of the apparently more paradoxical objections to utilitarianism, as when critics talk of a criminal's need or right to be punished. This is one of the anti-utilitarian themes in Dostoyevsky's portrait of Raskolnikov, where we are persuaded that he feels an overwhelming need to expiate his crime by undergoing punishment. One may come to think this merely part of Dostoyevsky's private world, described with such power that one momentarily took it to be how the real world is. Philosophers have pointed out that there is something paradoxical in a desire for punishment of which most criminals are unaware, or a right to it which most of them would willingly forgo. But this dismissal is too brisk. While no doubt few people desire punishment, many are distressed if not treated as responsible agents. A refusal to punish someone can constitute a denial of his status as a responsible agent. A team of Massachusetts psychiatrists wrote about a convicted murderer: 'We find Mr Cooper an interesting challenge in addition to being genuinely interested in him as a human being. Our impression is that he is quite treatable and might someday be a useful member of society.'[1] To see someone as 'treatable' or as 'an interesting challenge' may be well-intentioned, but it is not to see him as one's equal as a responsible agent. It is intelligible that people who are not mentally ill should sometimes prefer punishment to this sort of patronizing humanitarianism.[2]

But when some methods of preventing crime other than by

1 Quoted in Szasz, *Law, Liberty and Psychiatry*, 1963, Ch. 12.
2 Mr Derek Parfit has pointed out to me that in a world without blame the objection on the grounds of not being treated as an equal would collapse.

punishment are described as 'manipulation', it is unclear exactly what this charge comes to. Criticisms of advertising, propaganda, bribery, blackmail, 'behaviour therapy' as a treatment for neuroses and of Brave New World, often take the form of accusations that people are being manipulated. But, if rational discussion of these matters is to be sustained, it is necessary not to allow the emotional overtones of the word 'manipulation' to blind us to its diversity of application.

One type of manipulation can easily be described. This involves influencing someone's behaviour in such a way that he has no means of knowing what is causing him to act in the way he does. To make a man do something by means of subliminal advertising, post-hypnotic suggestion or certain types of drug is normally to manipulate him in this way. While it is true that someone with great experience of post-hypnotic suggestion or subliminal advertising may be able to guess that one of these is responsible for an apparently random impulse he feels, the great majority of people is unused to these techniques and, without being told, has no means of detecting their influence.

A milder form of manipulation includes all other kinds of non-rational persuasion. Much propaganda and normal advertising falls under this category, as does 'behaviour therapy': the application of conditioning techniques in an attempt to alter a pattern of behaviour. The type of persuasion in question is non-rational in that no attempt is made to argue that what is advertised is helpful to people: instead, associations are created in people's minds that in no way reflect real causal or logical relationships. When posters advertising cigarettes depict love scenes, or election notices bear photographs of a happy family enjoying a picnic, the means of persuasion are similar in principle to behaviour therapy. When the behaviour therapist attempts to stop someone smoking by making him sick every time he has a cigarette, the treatment is on the basis of a purely non-rational association: there is no suggestion that in daily life cigarettes are likely to cause sickness. This is also true of the very different association that the cigarette advertiser wishes to create. In real life smoking no more brings about sexual gratification than politicians bring about picnics. The advertiser is not like someone who makes a false claim in a discussion: the type of advertising under consideration is manipulation because no claim is specifically made. The advertiser hopes the association will be made, but not consciously subjected to examination.

Sometimes accusations of manipulation refer not to the method of persuasion but to its aim. To persuade someone to act in a certain way by means of blackmail is a kind of manipulation, but it is not included in either of the categories mentioned above. A man influenced by blackmail is normally aware of this influence, and the persuasion is in one sense perfectly rational. The association he makes between refusal to obey the blackmailer and subsequent physical assault or public disgrace may correspond exactly to the facts of the situation: the blackmailer may carry out his threats. The key feature of this form of manipulation is not that the actions advocated are not rational means to the ends of the agent, but rather that the agent is provided with new ends in order to further the aims of the manipulator. The blackmailer furthers his own aims by providing his victim with a new end: that of avoiding the threatened unpleasantness.

This kind of manipulation is not only to be found in cases of blackmail or bribery. There are many other ways in which someone can further his own aims by providing other people with new objectives. This is perhaps the main feature that distinguishes indoctrination from education. An educator is not debarred from putting forward his own views, or those of his party or church, but his long term aim will be to further the child's own interests by providing him with the critical equipment to judge those views for himself. An indoctrinator, on the other hand, puts first his own aim of propagating a particular set of views, and tries to instil into the child the pattern of values and aims he considers desirable, giving at best a lower priority to the development of powers of critical thought. It may be objected that indoctrination is often carried out by people who believe that it is in the best interests of the person they are indoctrinating. If one considers one knows the truth about religion, morals or politics, one may think that the end of communicating this truth can justifiably be given first priority, and hence that the development of critical thought is of lesser importance. But even where the aims of the indoctrinator are altruistic, they are still his own aims, and not (at least before the indoctrination) either the present aims of his victim, or a way of realizing those present aims. It is true that educators are concerned with stimulating people to adopt new aims, as well as with imparting means of realizing present ones. But in accordance with the priorities that distinguish him from the indoctrinator, the educator prefers a rationally argued rejection of the proffered new aims to an uncritical acceptance of them. He is primarily concerned to help people discover what they want to do, while even a benevolent indoctrinator will put other aims of his own first. High-minded indoctrination is still a kind of manipulation.

It is a distaste for this third kind of manipulation that underlies much criticism of advertising. Some advertising that is neither subliminal nor based on non-rational associations is still open to the charge of manipulating people by creating in them for commercial gain desires that they would not otherwise have. The suggestion is that advertisements do not merely provide us with information about the different products we can buy, but often also deliberately create artificial or 'synthesized' wants for products that do not satisfy any of our natural desires.[1] This view as it stands is open to the objection that there is no clear way of distinguishing between wants that are natural and wants that are artificial, and to the further objection that, if there is such a distinction, there seems no reason to suppose that the creation of artificial wants is of itself undesirable. It has been pointed out that the desires for sanitation and for museums are in their different ways created rather than natural wants.[2]

But the opposition to this kind of advertising need not rest on any dubious distinction between natural and artificial desires. The central feature that makes this advertising a kind of manipulation is that it creates desires that were not previously present (but not therefore any less 'natural') for the commercial gain of the advertiser. It is in aim that advertising is distinguished from the education that creates new desires for sanitation or for museums, or a new desire to see *King Lear*. If the main aim of the advertisement was to benefit the public by providing them with a new desire to try a new form of biscuit, this would not be manipulation. But it is, because the purpose of creating the new desire is to further the aims of someone else. The educator is distinguished both from the indoctrinator and the advertiser in that his main aim is to show people what can be gained from, say, *King*

1 Cf. Galbraith, *The Affluent Society*, 1958, Ch. 11.
2 Both these objections are made by Professor Richard Wollheim, *Socialism and Culture*, 1961.

Lear, so that they are in a position to make an informed choice as to whether this is the kind of play they like. He does not have as his main aim the creation of large audiences whenever *King Lear* is performed.

From the description of only these three varieties of manipulation, one can see that it is unplausible to suggest that all manipulation of people is to be avoided at all costs. It is hard to see what reasonable objection there could be to voluntary submission to the non-rational persuasive techniques of behaviour therapy in order to cure one's neurosis. Objections are more plausible where the conditioning is not voluntarily undertaken. One may object either on the grounds of disapproving of what people are being persuaded of or to do, or else on the basis of a belief in the desirability of persuasion being carried out openly and rationally. Objections to the form of manipulation that involves giving new desires or ends to someone else in order to further one's own aims are likely to be based on some principle similar to Kant's: 'all rational beings come under the law that each of them must treat itself and all others never merely as means, but in every case at the same time as ends in themselves'.

In the approach to punishment proposed here, it would be possible to build in restrictions to operate against all those kinds of manipulation that harm people. If one thinks, as one surely can, that it would be harmful to children (or adults) if they were made to hold moral beliefs by means of drugs, hypnosis or subliminal advertising, it is possible to argue against experimenting with these techniques. One might also, on similar grounds, restrict the use of other, less hidden, non-rational techniques of persuasion, such as behaviour therapy. (Though one may sometimes feel that some non-rational means of persuasion are harmless, or alternatively that the objections to some forms of crime are stronger than the objections to non-rational persuasion.)

The third type of manipulation mentioned involves giving someone new aims in order to further the aims of someone else, as in blackmail and in some types of indoctrination. This is the kind of manipulation that may involve breaking the rather obscure Kantian rule that we should never treat people 'merely as means'. It is sometimes suggested that the replacement of punishment by other forms of treatment is a policy open to criticism on these grounds. If this objection is well founded, it is necessary to weigh up the benefits to be gained by the policy, and to decide whether or not the use of these means would be too high a price to pay.

But, when the proposed policy is compared to that followed at present, the objection that it would involve this form of manipulation seems artificial. For our present policy is at least as much open to the same criticisms. At the moment, we send a man to prison, not in order to benefit him, but in order to provide him and others with new aims, which will benefit the public by reducing the number of crimes. And, if the compulsory treatment proposed is hedged about with restrictions on the types of non-rational persuasion permitted, it can hardly be said that we are treating the offender *merely* as a means. And, if the objection is that we should never treat people even partly as a means, this seems to say that under no circumstances should we ever to any degree sacrifice one person's interests to those of a greater number of people. But this moral principle, which would involve opposing the detention of a dangerous murderer against his will, is unlikely to commend itself to many.

6 WHOM SHOULD WE PUNISH?

Given the existence of a penal system and its techniques of punishment, what arguments can be invoked to defend the punishment of a particular person? Such a defence normally cites the aims used to justify punishment as an institution. Where someone has broken the law, people argue for his punishment on the familiar grounds of retribution, denunciation, reform, deterrence or the need to avoid unofficial retaliation.

But some penal theorists who are willing to justify punishment by appealing to one or more of these aims are unwilling to allow the unrestricted pursuit of any of them, and thus propose principles restricting the application of punishment. Several of the above aims would allow or encourage punishment (or perhaps 'punishment') of people who have not broken the law.[1] The aim of making a person fear to commit future crime might make us

[1] A prison psychologist tells me that some prisoners believe that this happens now.

'punish', not only convicted criminals, but also those who seem very likely to become criminals. Already psychological tests given to children at the age of five or six are proving remarkably successful at predicting who will grow up to be a frequent lawbreaker.[1] It seems quite possible that future research might show that 'punishment' administered at some crucial stage of emotional development, before any crime had been committed, as a warning of what would follow any detected lawbreaking, would be an effective deterrent. (Whether or not it actually did so might depend on the type of 'punishment' used: some present punishments perhaps lead to resentment rather than to fear of repetition, let alone to any kind of 'reform'.) And where the 'punishment' took the form of loss of liberty, this would effectively prevent the potential criminal from most kinds of lawbreaking during the period of his sentence. As mentioned in a previous chapter, 'punishment' of the innocent might help in reducing the number of crimes committed by others. It might do this by increasing the general fear of being caught or of being punished, or by helping to convince potential criminals of the wickedness of the offence. Or it might succeed by other means, as when the relations of a criminal are officially 'punished', as well as the offender himself. This technique is thought to provide potential criminals with an even stronger motive for obeying the law: during the Second World War, sanctions were applied to the relatives of Russian soldiers taken prisoner by the enemy, in order to give the soldiers a further motive for avoiding capture. It might also be argued that there should sometimes be 'punishment' of an innocent man who was widely thought to have broken the law, in order to protect him from unofficial retaliation.

With arguments of this sort in mind, some of those who oppose the legal infliction of suffering on innocent people have proposed the principle of 'retribution in distribution', according to which legal punishment may only be given to an offender, and then only for an offence which he could help committing. Such a principle can be defended either on grounds of justice, or else on the grounds that it leads either to some general social benefit or to the avoidance of some undesirable state of affairs.

Professor Hart has argued for a principle of this kind on both these grounds. His appeal to justice is stated as a 'doctrine of fair

1 Cf. S. and E. T. Glueck, *Predicting Delinquency and Crime*, 1959.

opportunity', which says that 'unless a man has the capacity and a fair opportunity or chance to adjust his behaviour to the law its penalties ought not to be applied to him'.[1] Here the relevant conception of fairness is a retributive one, but this doctrine is quite independent of the view that retribution is one of the justifying aims of a penal system. It is also independent of another retributive principle that clashes with one of the restrictions advocated earlier: this other retributive principle being that no one who has voluntarily broken the law should ever be allowed to escape punishment.

The other type of argument used here by Hart appeals to considerations of general social utility rather than to any principle of justice. He says that

> the system which makes liability to the law's sanctions dependent upon a voluntary act not only maximizes the power of the individual to determine by his choice his future fate; it also maximizes his power to identify in advance the space which will be left open to him free from the law's interference. Whereas a system from which responsibility was eliminated so that he was liable for what he did by mistake or accident would leave each individual not only less able to exclude the future interference by the law with his life, but also less able to foresee the times of the law's interference.[2]

Hart also says that our present system of responsibility is one in which

> even if things go wrong, as they do when mistakes are made or accidents occur, a man whose choices are right and who has done his best to keep the law will not suffer. . . . Our

---

1 'Punishment and the Elimination of Responsibility', Hobhouse Memorial Trust Lecture, 1962; reprinted in Hart, *Punishment and Responsibility*, 1968, p. 181. For the principle of justice that 'the more difficult it was for the person who undergoes a loss to have avoided the loss, the greater the weight that should be attached to that loss', cf. Haksar, 'Responsibility', *Proceedings of the Aristotelian Society*, Supplementary Volume 1966. This principle is rejected by C. H. Whitely in the same symposium.

2 *Punishment and Responsibility*, 1968, p. 181–182. This is a consideration, but surely not a very powerful one. There are many other unpredictable interferences with our lives, which we regret, but not enough to do much about. Why should unpredictable interference by the law be so much worse?

system does not interfere till harm has been done and has been proved to have been done with the appropriate *mens rea*. But the risk that is here taken is not taken for nothing. It is the price we pay for general recognition that a man's fate should depend upon his choice and this is to foster the prime social virtue of self-restraint.[1]

Hart says that underlying these points is the important general principle that in human society we interpret each other's movements as expressions of choices, and it is of crucial importance to social relationships whether, for example, a blow was deliberate or involuntary. He says,

> If as our legal moralists maintain it is important for the law to reflect common judgments of morality, it is surely even more important that it should in general reflect in its judgments on human conduct distinctions which not only underly morality, but pervade the whole of our social life. This it would fail to do if it treated men merely as alterable, predictable, curable or manipulable things.

Hart recognizes that the arguments for the principle of retribution in distribution need not persuade us to accept it as a principle that should not in any circumstances be infringed, for he reminds us to recognize cases where it secures minimal benefits at too great a social cost.

The general underlying principle that Hart cites in defence of the requirement of *mens rea* is obscure. It is true that we do in social life attach importance to the intentions underlying actions, and that it is on these for the most part that our reactive attitudes depend. But it is surely unplausible to suggest that the law should be guided by certain distinctions simply because they 'pervade the whole of our social life'. It seems more reasonable to suggest that people should be treated as much as possible as responsible agents because this is in itself desirable, rather than because such treatment is deeply ingrained in other areas of our social life. And the ambiguities of speaking of treating people 'merely as . . . manipulable things' have already been mentioned. It does not seem that all forms of manipulation are in themselves objectionable. And, as with the similar Kantian point about not treating

1 *Ibid.,* p. 182.

people merely as means, it is unclear just how much consideration one has to give to interests of the person being manipulated before one stops treating him as 'merely manipulable'.

But, despite these difficulties, one can make out a case for the principle of retribution in distribution. It is possible to defend it, not only by invoking Hart's other arguments, but also by arguing that to abandon it would involve objectionable forms of manipulation. One kind of manipulation, to which objection seems reasonable, is to treat a person in a way that alters his behaviour in a way advantageous to other people, without any regard to his own interests. The principle of retribution in distribution is one safeguard against this. If we have to retain punishments for some offences, or if the alternative of compulsory treatment is unpleasant or unwanted, we should not be willing to use these means of altering a person's behaviour without any regard to his interests. One way in which we can manifest a regard for his interests is by giving him an opportunity to avoid punishment by obeying the law. We are not manipulating people, treating them merely as means, if we make it clear that in general they will only have to submit to punishment or reformative treatment as a result of actions that they could freely have chosen not to perform. It may be that with some crimes, the social grounds for a system of strict liability, flouting the principle of retribution in distribution, will be too strong to ignore. In these cases, the situation will be similar to cases where people with dangerous infectious diseases are compulsorily isolated, regardless of the fact that they probably could not help getting the disease. But, if one cares about not treating people merely as means, one will place the onus of argument on the defenders of strict liability in any given case.

It has been suggested by Dr Nigel Walker[1] that it is a mistake to think of the principle of retribution in distribution as a 'morally binding principle', but that we should rather think of it as a 'practically desirable one'. He says that 'it is important to realize that the strongest case for this sophisticated form of retributivism is not that to breach it occasionally is unthinkable or morally insupportable, but that to abandon it completely is politically out of the question'. Walker's argument for denying that the principle is morally binding is based on instances where we feel

1 'The Aims of a Penal System', The James Seth Memorial Lecture, 1966.

entitled to disobey it. If we have extremely good reasons for supposing that a man will murder or mutilate someone, we are prepared to impose detention on him although he has not yet broken the law. Walker says that at present we deal with such cases by a kind of 'double-think'. If the man is mentally abnormal, we have him detained in a mental hospital, and salve our consciences by saying that mental hospitals are not part of the penal system. Or if he is too sane for this, we wait for him to commit some technical 'breach of the peace' and then have him 'bound over to keep the peace'. Walker points out that we also often penalize negligence, even where this has caused no harm, as may be the case where someone is punished for driving without due care and attention. And there are the offences of strict liability, so that a shopkeeper, for example, commits an offence if he sells adulterated food even if he has no way of telling that it is adulterated, as in the case of tinned food.

But these instances need not lead us to Walker's conclusion that political considerations are the main justification for obeying the principle of retribution in distribution. In the first place it is necessary to distinguish between the different types of case where Walker claims the principle is breached. It can be argued that the punishment of negligence, unlike offences of strict liability, can be reconciled with Hart's principle. If I drive a car without due care and attention, I am not in the same situation as a shopkeeper selling tinned food that is adulterated, for I am in a position to conform to the law. It is not true that whenever one is negligent one cannot help being so.[1] And, turning from negligence to Walker's most plausible example, the case of the potential murderer is surely just the sort of case Hart must have had in mind when he admitted that sometimes the high social cost of adhering to the principle might justify our not doing so. But this does not remove the principle from the realm of morality to the realm of political expediency. Walker presents us with the alternative that we are dealing either with a 'morally binding' principle or else with a

[1] Cf. Hart, 'Negligence, *Mens Rea*, and Criminal Responsibility', in Guest, *Oxford Essays in Jurisprudence*, 1961; reprinted in Hart, *Punishment and Responsibility*, 1968. The claim that there is a prima facie inconsistency between arguments used against strict liability offences and a willingness to allow punishment for negligence is made by Wasserstrom, 'Strict Liability in the Criminal Law', *Stanford Law Review*, 1960; reprinted in Thomson and Dworkin (eds.), *Ethics*, 1968.

'practically desirable' one. But it is not absurd to speak of a moral principle that admits of exceptions: all that is important is that one should be able to justify the exceptions on other moral grounds.

The question 'whom should we punish?' brings up the problem of collective responsibility. It is possible to argue in favour of punishing someone, not because he himself committed the offence, but because he is a member of a group that is held to have done so. Thus it might be thought reasonable when giving out punishments for the Nazi crimes to punish any member of the German government of the period, or any very senior party official, even if there were no evidence that he took an active part in proposing or carrying out the policy of genocide. And some people go so far as to hold all or almost all the German people of the time responsible for that policy, and would perhaps have supported some collective punishment, had that been feasible.

Many people oppose any doctrine of collective responsibilty on the grounds that it is unjust to blame or punish individuals who took no part in the action or policy carried out by other people who happened to belong to the same group. But it is important to distinguish here between the question of whether it is wrong to punish or blame people whose only crime was indifference or lack of opposition, and the separate question of whether it is wrong to blame or punish one person for the acts of another. The relatively passive senior Nazi official may be held to have been at least culpably negligent, if one considers that his position was such that he had either special knowledge of the policy or else a degree of influence that he should have used to oppose the policy. And whether or not one holds an ordinary citizen responsible may again depend on the degree of knowledge that one judges was available to him, and on the extent to which one thinks that the evil of the policy makes inactivity amount to culpable negligence. Where one thinks that the inaction of officials or of ordinary citizens amounted to culpable negligence on the part of each one of them, then collective responsibility raises no special difficulties of its own. It only raises special problems where it involves blaming or punishing a whole group of people, some of whom neither did what was wrong, nor behaved in a culpably negligent way. In such a case, collective responsibility is open to criticism based on the principle of retribution in distribution. But in the former type of case, collective punishment is no harder to justify than individual punishment for actions or for negligence.

The view being defended here is that it is desirable not to 'punish' someone either for a crime he has not committed, or for a crime that he could not help committing. This policy can be defended both on grounds of justice and on the grounds, stressed by Hart, of maximizing freedom and of fostering self-restraint. But the principle that punishment should not be applied in such cases may come into conflict with the aim of reducing the number of crimes committed. Then one can only choose between the rival aims on the grounds of their relative importance in the situation in question. There are two key problems posed by this doctrine of retribution in distribution. One is this moral question of when there are sufficiently good social reasons for over-riding it. The other concerns the most appropriate mechanism by which a legal decision can be reached as to whether or not someone could help breaking the law.

7 OVER-RIDING THE PRINCIPLE OF RETRIBUTION IN DISTRIBUTION

It may be that, in very exceptional cases, a judge would be morally justified in over-riding the principle of retribution in distribution to the extent of punishing a man who has not broken the law. But such cases seem only likely to arise where there is a serious threat of lynch law. For the most part, the arguments against inflicting sanctions on the innocent will presumably be found very much stronger than any other considerations.

But, for legislators, the problem of when to flout the principle of retribution in distribution is more often a pressing one. The legislator has to decide whether or not to make a crime one of strict liability, so that some or all of the pleas made by saying 'I could not help it' will not be recognized as excusing the offender from punishment.

There is a case for distinguishing here between pleas of no act and of unintentional act, on the one hand, and pleas of excusable intentional act on the other. Where either of the first two kinds of plea are made, unless the unintentional act is the result of negligence, there is a strong presumption in favour of adhering to the principle of retribution in distribution. Punishment in such cases is quite unfair, and only seems justified where the crime is very harmful, and where, at the same time, making it a crime of strict liability will considerably reduce its occurrence.[1]

Why might there not be the same presumption against punishing someone who can make a plea of excusing circumstances or of unalterable intention? For anyone who believes in the principle of retribution in distribution, there is a presumption against punishing anyone who could not help breaking the law. But, where the illegal act was performed intentionally, there may be stronger grounds than in other cases for flouting the principle. One reason for this can be seen by considering the numbers of persistent criminals who may act under the influence of some mental disorder, and could reasonably make a plea of unalterable intention. Mr Tony Parker's classic description of 'Charlie Smith' shows us a persistent offender who has never been absolved from legal responsibility for his crimes, and yet who obviously has certain psychological incapacities.[2] Information about his inadequate upbringing, about his limited opportunities to find a tolerable way of life when coming out of prison, and evidence about his personality derived from interviews, all make it highly unplausible that Charlie Smith was open to persuasion to give up his life of petty crime. This impression is reinforced by his history, where eight convictions had resulted in total sentences of twenty-six years, with an average period of freedom between sentences of only eleven weeks. Charlie Smith seems far more representative of persistent offenders than one might suppose. Concluding a survey of a hundred recidivist prisoners, Dr D. J. West writes

> The incidence of psychiatric symptoms was much higher than anticipated. Ten per cent were or had been psychotic and a further sixteen per cent had been admitted to hospital or discharged from the forces on psychiatric grounds. Altogether, at least a third had a history of severe mental disorder.[3]

1   This is the case that can be made in defence of strict liability in the law relating to driving with excessive alcohol in one's blood. It seems harder to make out such a case for strict liability in the law relating (e.g.) to the selling of adulterated food.
2   *The Unknown Citizen,* 1963.   3   *The Habitual Prisoner,* 1963, Ch. 10.

This raises a serious problem for supporters of the view that those who cannot help what they do should not be subject to legal sanctions. For, if Dr West's sample is representative, about a third of the most persistent criminals who are caught stand some chance of being included among those who acted as the result of psychological disability. If we adhere very strictly to the principle that the law should not interfere in the lives of such people, we are likely to deprive ourselves of any chance of eliminating a very large proportion of the crimes that are committed. No doubt our present penal treatment of men like Charlie Smith manages to be both unfair and ineffective. But it should not be beyond our powers to devise a form of compulsory treatment sufficiently humane and effective to make the unfairness worth while. Hopelessly inadequate people might benefit from a form of probation, very different from what we now have, where very great supervision would be exercised over their lives. They might be compelled to take certain jobs, and in some cases to live in certain hostels. Instead of the withering of necessary social skills that now takes place in prison, they could learn, under close supervision, how to adapt themselves better to the ordinary world of having a regular job.

A policy of this sort might be defended, not as punishment, but on paternalist grounds as a promising form of treatment for some of those with psychological disabilities. But even where one is reluctant to invoke paternalist arguments in favour of such compulsory supervision, it can be defended as a penal policy whose effectiveness would outweigh the objections to applying compulsion to offenders who could not help what they did. Again, experiment is needed to see how effective such a policy would be. There is no general answer (other than a vacuous one) to the question 'when should we over-ride the principle of retribution in distribution?' We should only do so when the moral gains outweigh the moral losses. And when is that? The answer to this question depends partly on one's moral attitudes. But it also depends partly on information as to the effectiveness of alternative responses to crime. We lack this information because of the timidity and unimaginativeness of our legislators.

8 LEGAL MECHANISMS: PUNISHMENT AND TREATMENT

Lady Wootton has written as follows:

> ... *mens rea* has, so to speak – and this is the crux of the matter – *got into the wrong place*. Traditionally, the requirement of the guilty mind is written into the actual definition of a crime. No guilty intention, no crime, is the rule. Obviously this makes sense if the law's concern is with wickedness: where there is no guilty intention, there can be no wickedness. But it is equally obvious, on the other hand, that an action does not become innocuous merely because whoever performed it meant no harm. If the object of the criminal law is to prevent the occurrence of socially damaging actions, it would be absurd to turn a blind eye to those which were due to carelessness, negligence or even accident. The question of motivation is *in the first instance* irrelevant.
>
> But only in the first instance. At a later stage, that is to say, after what is now known as a conviction, the presence or absence of guilty intention is all-important for its effect on the appropriate measures to be taken to prevent a recurrence of the forbidden act. The prevention of accidental deaths presents different problems from those involved in the prevention of wilful murders.[1]

Lady Wootton advocates this kind of 'disregard of responsibility', and says that

> one of the most important consequences must be to obscure the present rigid distinction between the penal and the medical institution. .... The formal distinction between prison and hospital will become blurred, and, one may reasonably expect, eventually obliterated altogether. Both will be simply 'places of safety' in which offenders receive the treatment which experience suggests is most likely to evoke the desired response.[2]

Since Lady Wootton assumes that punishment is at least in part

1 *Crime and the Criminal Law,* 1963, Ch. 2.   2 *Ibid.,* Ch. 3.

retributive in aim, it is understandable that her own utilitarian approach should lead her to hope that one day punishment will be wholly replaced by treatment. But we have seen that a utilitarian policy for reducing crime might involve 'treatment' that was unwanted or unpleasant, either where the aim is to 'cure' the offender or to deter other potential offenders. It is in this context that one sees the value of Professor Hart's principle of 'retribution in distribution'. In the light of this principle, how can one evaluate Lady Wootton's desire to eliminate the distinction between the penal and the medical institution?

In one respect at least, Lady Wootton's proposals threaten our aim that we should normally not impose suffering on someone for an act that they could not help. In our own society, there is a very real stigma attached to 'what is now known as a conviction'. Anyone convicted of a crime is in danger of some degree of social disapproval, and for many this may be one of the most unpleasant of the consequences of being caught breaking the law. Under a system where someone who could not help his act is not convicted, he is spared this stigma. Under Lady Wootton's proposed system, he would very likely not be spared this. It may be said in reply to this that, under Lady Wootton's system, stigma would disappear altogether. But it is not clear that the stigma attached to proved law-breaking would disappear merely because this was followed by something called 'treatment' rather than by something called 'punishment'. (In some circles those who have been in a mental hospital carry a greater stigma than those who have been in prison.)[1] And it may be that the social stigma attached to conviction plays an important part in deterring people from breaking the law. If this is so, we may have to weigh the desirability of eliminating this form of suffering against the harm caused by a possible increase in the crime rate. But even if it is both possible and desirable to remove the stigma that goes with conviction, it is clear that this will not happen overnight, so that, in the early stages of implementing Lady Wootton's proposals, some people would suffer in this way for acts they could not help.

A further objection to Lady Wootton's programme is that penal and medical policies may have radically different aims. The point

---

1 Cf. Dr Nigel Walker, 'Liberty, Liability, Culpability', in Craft, *Psychopathic Disorders,* 1966. For a suggestive discussion of many aspects of stigma, cf. Goffman, *Stigma: Notes on the Management of Spoiled Identity,* 1963.

of medicine is to benefit the person who receives it, while the point of penal treatment can be at least as much, or even entirely, to benefit other people by reducing the amount of crime. Sometimes a medical cure can benefit people other than the person cured, who may then be less of a nuisance, and sometimes successful penal treatment may benefit the criminal. Sometimes the most effective penal treatment may be compulsory medical treatment. But the fact that two ends can sometimes be realized by the same means does not mean that they should be kept distinct. The possible separateness of penal and medical aims is important here because their realization can be limited by quite different sets of principles. Compulsory penal treatment may be justified by appealing to the interest of the community, while compulsory medical treatment may be justified on paternalist grounds. From some moral standpoints one could argue that we should be far more reluctant to intervene on paternalist grounds than in the interests of the community, and from other standpoints one could argue for exactly the reverse priorities. Both these types of view would automatically be denied application in a system that did not recognize the distinction upon which they are based. Lady Wootton's proposals assume that these views can be brushed aside, and this assumption is one we may well be reluctant to accept.

If one wishes to retain the principle that, unless there are strong grounds for their being so treated, people who cannot help their illegal acts should not be subjected to legal penalties, there remains the problem of devising the most appropriate legal mechanism for this. The serious difficulties here do not arise in cases of unintentional acts, but rather in cases of intentional acts resulting from psychological incapacity.

Detailed consideration of legal procedure is not part of the task of a book such as this. I am only concerned to argue for the acceptance of certain guiding principles. So far as the mechanism of exempting the psychologically inadequate is concerned, some of the relevant general principles can be briefly stated. One is that, in questions of psychological capacity, psychiatrists are the best experts we have, and such matters should be decided by them outside the court, rather than by a jury. (Such a system would give considerable power to possibly prejudiced psychiatrists. Our present system gives the same power to possibly prejudiced jurymen.)¹ Another guiding principle, argued for in the previous chapter, is that the law should put to the panel of psychiatrists a general question about impaired capacities, rather than a question phrased in terms of particular diagnostic categories.

Finally, the question put to the psychiatrists should be less general than 'could he help what he did?' or 'could he have acted otherwise?' As we have seen, 'he could not help it' is a phrase that can be used to make a number of different kinds of claim, and it is undesirable to ask psychiatrists a question that they might answer, say, in the light of hazy notions about determinism. Where a man intentionally performed an act that was illegal, it may be helpful to ask the psychiatrists whether he could have been persuaded to act differently, as a clarification supplementary to a question asking whether he lacked the capacity to act differently. It may be that our knowledge is at present so limited that we are bound to be unable to decide with certainty to what extent a person's capacities are impaired. If so, this is a problem that philosophical refinement of the questions to be asked cannot alone overcome. But the account of 'unalterable intention' proposed previously does give some guidance as to the type of question that is relevant. ('Unalterable intention' seems a less unhappy phrase than 'irresistible impulse', with its suggestion of acting only on the spur of the moment.)

As our psychiatric knowledge advances, we may find that in other parts of human behaviour we are able to recognize many states where the ability to respond to persuasion is as clearly impaired as it is in the alcoholic. In our present state of knowledge it is at least worth asking the right kind of question, even if we must now be satisfied with answers that are plausible rather than conclusive. It is true that, since 'being open to persuasion' is a matter of degree, there will be disagreements as to the degree to which persuasion must be ineffective for a plea of unalterable intention to be acceptable. But that it is a matter of degree is, as we

---

1 This principle was rejected in the *Report of the Royal Commission on Capital Punishment*, 1953, which said that the question of responsibility 'is essentially a moral question ... to whose solution medicine can bring valuable aid, and it is one which is most appropriately decided by a jury of ordinary men and women, not by medical or legal experts'. (Para. 283.) It has been argued in this book that the question of which criteria of responsibility to adopt is a moral one. But the question of whether they are satisfied is a factual question, even if a rather difficult one.

have seen, not peculiar to this plea, but also applies to many pleas of no action, unintentional action (to the extent that what counts as negligence is a matter of dispute) and of excusing circumstances. If one cares about not punishing those who could not help doing what they did, one may well wish to see a policy of treating dubious borderline cases generously.

9

MORALITY AND EVASION

Antiquated and inapplicable norms, modes of thought, and
theories are likely to degenerate into ideologies whose
function it is to conceal the actual meaning of conduct
rather than to reveal it.

Karl Mannheim: *Ideology and Utopia.*

Common-sense is part of the home-made ideology of those
who have been deprived of fundamental learning, of those
who have been kept ignorant. This ideology is compounded
from different sources: items that have survived from religion, items of empirical knowledge, items of protective
scepticism, items culled for comfort from the superficial
learning that *is* supplied. But the point is that common-
sense can never teach itself, can never advance beyond its
own limits, for as soon as the lack of fundamental learning
has been made good, all items become questionable and the
whole function of common-sense is destroyed. Common-
sense can only exist as a category insofar as it can be
distinguished from the spirit of enquiry, from philosophy.

John Berger: *A Fortunate Man.*

At his trial in Jerusalem, Eichmann tried to excuse the part he
played in the Nazi murders by saying that he had only obeyed
orders from above. We may be uncertain how true this claim was,

but most of us condemn his role even if he only obeyed instructions and did not initiate policy. Even if he did not fully recognize the wrongness of what he was doing, we do not on this account excuse him. This is because we believe that he was not mentally ill, and had the capacity to see his actions for what they were. To 'overlook' such results as flowed from his obedience would be extreme self-deception.

It is sometimes held that there are difficulties about holding someone responsible for what he does in a state of self-deception. It is suggested that we must find some special grounds for excluding such a state from the kinds of ignorance that excuse acts. But to describe a man's state as self-deception is already to mark it off from other states of ignorance or lack of awareness. My ignorance of my exact height does not amount to self-deception, since I have no reason to suppose that to know it would be in any way unpleasant. But, if I usually eat too much, my exact weight may be something I would prefer not to know, and my ignorance of that may be self-deception. Yet, not all ignorance of unpalatable facts counts as self-deception. If I could find out for certain the date of my death, this would very likely give me a nasty shock, especially if it were nearer than I hoped. But my ignorance of this date is not the result of self-deception, since this is not information that I can find out. Ignorance must be avoidable, and reasonably readily avoidable, before it can be attributed to self-deception. How readily avoidable the ignorance must be depends upon the importance of the matter. In this way, self-deception can be assimilated to a kind of negligence. Where one negligently fails to do something, one has fallen below a standard that one could reasonably be expected to satisfy, and the amount of trouble or effort that can reasonably be demanded of one varies with the importance of what is at stake.

If Eichmann was in a state of ignorance of the moral criticisms that could have been made of his acts, this amounted to self-deception, since two crucial conditions were satisfied. The ignorance, if it existed, must surely have resulted from a refusal to raise certain questions, which was motivated by an awareness that the answers would have been unpalatable. (The distaste for probable answers must play a causal role if the failure to raise the questions is to count as self-deception.) And the ignorance could have been avoided without unreasonable trouble or effort.[1] This condition, in the case of Eichmann, is massively over-satisfied: the matter was so important that an enormous amount of thought on his part could reasonably have been demanded, and very little thought would have brought the moral criticisms to mind. On this view of self-deception, there seems no special objection to blaming a self-deceiver, over and above any general doubts about blaming people for negligence.

If we assume that Eichmann realized the wrongness of what he did, few morally interesting consequences follow from our condemnation of him.[2] But many of us would consider him blameworthy if, as the result of certain kinds of negligence, he was unaware of the wrongness of what he did. It may be objected that to speak of Eichmann's acts in terms of 'negligence' or of being 'unaware' is absurd. No doubt it would be absurd to suggest that a man in Eichmann's position was unaware of the deaths to which he made so large a contribution. But he might, as a result of self-deception, have become insensitive to the moral criticisms that could be made of what he was doing. Such self-deception might involve a refusal to let his thoughts dwell on the fate of his victims, or perhaps the adoption of a belief that one has an absolute duty to obey orders, which must over-ride any moral scruples one may have. I do not claim that this was Eichmann's state of mind. But, if he was in such a state of self-deception, we need not concede that this is any way absolves him from blame.

This willingness to blame Eichmann for what he did, even if he was unaware how wrong it was, is a moral attitude with which it is possible to disagree. It may be said that, if we are not willing to hold a psychopath responsible for his actions, it is inconsistent to hold Eichmann responsible for what he did in partial unawareness of its wrongness. But this charge of inconsistency depends either upon a misunderstanding of why we should be reluctant to punish psychopaths, or else upon ignorance of what psychopathy is held to be. A prime reason for not holding

1 I am unsure to what extent this account of self-deception resembles Professor Fingarette's account of it as involving a 'splitting of the ego'. Cf. his *Self-Deception,* 1969.

2 But should there not be some practical consequences? We make heavy demands on people when, in the spirit of Nuremberg, we demand that they disobey orders. It seems only reasonable that we should set up international legal bodies to which people in such a situation could appeal for protection, over the heads of their own government.

psychopaths responsible can be stated in Bradley's words: 'Responsibility implies a *moral* agent. No one is accountable, who is not capable of knowing (not, who does not know) the moral quality of his acts.' It is this distinction between actually knowing and being capable of knowing the moral quality of one's acts that is crucial here. Those who have studied psychopaths sometimes produce evidence that they have impaired capacities, which can be identified independently of their harmful actions. It is because of evidence, either that they are incapable of controlling their actions or that they are incapable of grasping the moral quality of what they do, that we should be disinclined to treat psychopaths as responsible agents. Had evidence of this kind been forthcoming about Eichmann, there would have been grounds for not holding him responsible. It appears that he was not a psychopath, but could have realized the wickedness of what he did.

Our moral condemnation of Eichmann, if independent of any belief that he appreciated the wrongness of what he did, must depend on the view that people sometimes have a duty to submit what they do to moral criticism. On this view, there is a kind of moral negligence, which consists not merely in failing to do what one believes one ought to do, but also in evading or refusing to raise questions about the morality of what one does. I shall argue here that inadequate or confused moral concepts can play a key part in the evasion of responsibility that consists in not raising certain questions. This is an example of the way in which certain concepts, at the heart of a social or personal system of beliefs, can function to cramp and distort our thinking.

1 TWO EVASIONS OF RESPONSIBILITY

If Eichmann held that the duty to obey orders was absolute, admitting of no moral criticism, this was not, and is not, a very rare view. There must be military academies throughout the world in which the denial of this view would be seen as eccentric, not to say disgraceful. At the 'Official Secrets' trial, in 1962, the following exchange is said to have taken place. One of the accused, Mr Pottle, asked the Air Commodore in the witness-box, 'Would you press the button you know is going to annihilate millions of people?' The reply was, 'If the circumstances demanded it, I would.'[1] It is hard to envisage any plausible situation in which, for a morality such as utilitarianism, there would be adequate grounds for the annihilation involved in nuclear war. It seems not unfair to guess that, in the Air Commodore's view, the relevant circumstances would be ones where either patriotic duty or obedience to orders was in question.

The doctrine that one's morality would permit the destruction of millions of people is an unappealing one. Instead, the alternative suggestion is made that obedience to orders or to the claims of patriotism involves a compliance that is outside the jurisdiction of morality. That any other view is virtually unintelligible was clearly implied by Lord Justice Parker in his question to journalists at the 'Vassall tribunal': 'How can you say there is any dishonour in you if you do what is your duty in the ordinary way as a citizen, in putting the interests of the state above everything?'[2] Among various alternative points of view is that expressed by E. M. Forster's remark: 'I hate the idea of causes, and if I had the choice of betraying my country or betraying my friend, I hope I should have the guts to betray my country.' There may be some case to be made for disagreeing with Mr Forster's choice, but there seems no case for implying that it is not a genuine moral option.

It is attractive to claim that one's morality can be stated in terms of such broad concepts as love, happiness, freedom or truthfulness. But it is often hard to justify, within such a widely conceived morality, a policy of universal obedience to orders, the law[3] or the demands of patriotism. Those with the habit of obedience may be tempted to escape from responsibility by treating their obedience as something inevitable and beyond question. In this way it is possible to overlook the extent to which our obedience depends on our own choice, and, as Eichmann may have done, to conceal from ourselves the nature of the voluntary harm we do.

1 Quoted in Stein (ed.), *Nuclear Weapons: A Catholic Response*, 1963.
2 Quoted in MacIntyre, *Secularization and Moral Change*, 1967.
3 For the difficulty of justifying unconditional obedience to law, cf. Wasserstrom, 'The Obligation to Obey the Law', *U.C.L.A. Law Review*, 1963; reprinted in Summers (ed.), *Essays in Legal Philosophy*, 1968. Unconvincing arguments in favour of unconditional obedience can be found in Plato's *Crito* and in many authoritarian philosophical works ever since.

Another attempted way of escape from moral responsibility is sometimes taken by those engaged in scientific research. This is to separate sharply 'pure' research from the uses made of the knowledge it brings, in such a way that the former is uncontaminated by moral criticism of the latter. This separation makes it impossible to criticize the act of undertaking any piece of pure research: one can only criticize the applications of science. This view is illustrated by Oppenheimer's remarks about the development of the atomic bomb:

> It is my judgment that in these things when you see something that is technically sweet you go ahead and do it and you argue about what to do about it only after you have had your technical success. That is the way it was with the atomic bomb. I do not think anybody opposed making it; there were some debates about what to do with it after it was made. [1]

Oppenheimer also said

> I did my job, which was the job I was supposed to do. I was not in a policy-making position at Los Alamos. I would have done anything that I was asked to do, including making the bombs a different shape, if I had thought it was technically feasible. [2]

One motive for trying to remove scientific research from the realm of moral choices may be the difficulty of the decisions that are demanded. It is often very hard to be sure how the work in a field may be used,[3] and, where there are various possible uses, it is hard to weigh up gains and losses. A discovery in biochemistry may be available both for the cure of a disease and for germ warfare. Discoveries in genetics will make it possible to avoid children being born deformed or feeble-minded, but they will also open up the possibility of Brave New World. A scientist who seriously raises the question of whether he ought to work in a particular field is faced with two problems. One is that of predicting what use will in fact be made of his work. The other is that of deciding how acceptable he finds that use.

1 Quoted in Jungk, *Brighter than a Thousand Suns,* Pelican Edition 1964, p. 266.
2 Quoted in Jungk, *op. cit.,* p. 292.
3 'If I had only known, I would have been a locksmith': Einstein.

The problems are parallel to those of a man at the start of a war who wonders whether or not he ought to be a pacifist. Unless he holds to some principle admitting of no exceptions, whether of patriotism or of the sanctity of life, he is likely to have to weigh up gains and losses for each of the two courses of action. There are factual questions of predicting how much harm the war will do, how much harm will be done if the wrong side wins, and how much difference either way will be made by his decision. Then there is the choice of one evil as less objectionable than the other. Apart from the difficulties of choice between evils, the making of the relevant predictions can seem an almost hopeless task. In 1939, could one be sure that the Second World War would last more than a year? Could one be sure that it would not last twenty years?

It is easy to see why scientists, whose success results partly from concentration on problems that should be soluble, may be reluctant to confront the more speculative issues raised by moral doubts. James Franck mentioned some of the principles of scientific method, in connection with the making of the atomic bomb:

> We scientists seem to be unable to apply these principles to the immensely complex problems of the political world and its social order. In general we are cautious and therefore tolerant and disinclined to accept total solutions. Our very objectivity prevents us from taking a strong stand in political differences, in which the right answer is never on one side. So we took the easiest way out and hid in our ivory tower. We felt that neither the good nor the evil applications were our responsibility.[1]

Yet the difficulty of making a moral decision does not automatically absolve one from responsibility for evading it, whether it is about fighting in war or about doing research. The evasion is perhaps excusable where the consequences that can be foreseen are slight, but the more serious those consequences, the more blameworthy the evasion will be.

But those who wish not to take responsibility for the consequences of their research do not always cite the difficulty of their predicament as an excuse. There are attempts at justification that

[1] Quoted in Jungk, *op. cit.*, p. 41.

can be offered.[1] There is the argument that 'if I don't do it, someone else will': an argument that, if accepted, would justify making gas for Belsen. Or there is the argument that, after the research has been done, there is an intervening decision by someone else as to whether or not to use it for bad purposes. It is suggested that the intervention of someone else's decision absolves the scientist from responsibility: we do not hold the maker of rat poison responsible for its use by a murderer. But this argument will not bear the weight often put on it: some research is simply on new means of destruction, with no possible 'good' use such as rat poison has. And it has to be argued for, rather than merely suggested, that making new discoveries available to politicians and the military is like selling rat poison at the chemist's to the general public, rather than like selling it to a homicidal fanatic. But the attempted justification may not consist in poor arguments, but in the mere assertion, as a piece of 'commonsense' not in need of defence, that pure science is a realm of its own, outside the jurisdiction of morality.

The attempts mentioned here to create realms of activity outside morality, are dependent upon an inadequate conception of morality.

2 MORAL BELIEFS

Which of one's beliefs are moral beliefs? In trying to lay down criteria by which to answer this question, there is a danger of making the concept of morality either too narrow or too broad. To say that a moral belief is one that is based on rules of conduct laid down by God, or else that it is one intended to direct conduct towards maximizing human happiness, is to rule out either all non-religious or all non-utilitarian moralities by definition. But if one is aware of the variety of moral codes, and aware of the need not to identify morality itself with one's own particular moral outlook, other difficulties arise.

If an anthropologist sets out to give an account of the moral

1 Cf. Tolstoy, *War and Peace,* 2nd Epilogue, Ch. 8: 'These justifications release those who produce the events from moral responsibility. These temporary aims are like the broom fixed in front of a locomotive to clear the snow from the rails in front: they clear men's moral responsibilities from their path.'

code of a group he is studying, there may be real problems in deciding which of their beliefs ought to be mentioned. There are various features of a belief that certain conduct is desirable that count in favour of classifying it as a moral one. Those who hold the belief may think it ought to be universally acted upon. More often than other beliefs, this one may provide a motive for acting against what are thought to be one's own interests. The belief may guide conduct in accordance with the commands of some being or institution held to have special authority. It may be based on some general considerations of the well-being of some large group of people, or of all humans, or of all conscious beings. Flouting the belief may give rise to feelings of guilt. The presence of any of these features may take it more rather than less plausible to see the belief as a moral one.

But none of these factors is either a necessary or a sufficient condition of a belief being part of someone's morality. I may hold a moral belief about how I ought to act without believing that anyone else in a relevantly similar situation ought to act in the same way. If those philosophers are correct who have argued that such beliefs are arbitrary, or in some way inconsistent, this only shows that some people have arbitrary or incoherent moral beliefs, not that such beliefs cannot be moral. On the other hand, I may hold that everyone ought to behave in a certain way, such as keeping their mouths closed when eating, but, far from this being one of my moral beliefs, I may regard it as merely a matter of etiquette, or at most an aesthetic preference. One can have moral beliefs that rarely conflict with self-interest and which have little to do with the commands of any authority or with the well-being of any group. The belief that homosexuality is wrong, not because it is harmful to people or forbidden by God, but because it is 'unnatural' is of this kind. One may believe in obeying the law, on the grounds that it has some special authority, and often do so against one's own interests, without this being among one's moral beliefs. I may think people ought to have plenty of exercise, because it is good for them, without seeing this as part of my morality. And there is no necessary link between moral beliefs and feelings of guilt. One might hold the moral principle that one ought always to obey the law, and yet feel no guilt on slightly exceeding the speed limit. On the other hand, it is possible to feel guilty on account of a mere breach of etiquette.

Perhaps there would be no general agreement among all those who use the word 'morality' upon its exact scope. Some newspapers appear to think that an issue is one of morality only if it concerns sex. But, where there are different ways of using a word, there can be grounds for saying that one way of using it is more useful than others. There is little to commend restricting the scope of the word to sexual affairs. But there is a strong case for including in the scope of morality only those beliefs that have a certain special importance or priority. For Kant, the ultimate basis of morality was the categorical imperative, and recent discussions of Kant's moral theory have dwelt on the content of this imperative. But it is worth paying attention to his description of it as categorical. Hypothetical imperatives tell you what to do in order to bring about something else: perhaps that you must hurry if you are to catch the train. But the categorical imperative simply tells you what to do. Whatever criticisms there may be of Kant's basic moral injunction, there is much to be said for defining morality in terms of being categorical. Moral beliefs are never justified by appealing to non-moral considerations alone, nor can any purely non-moral considerations justify flouting a moral belief about what one ought to do. This is the way in which moral considerations take priority over all others.[1]

To say that moral beliefs about what one ought to do have this kind of priority is not to say that one always, or even usually, acts on them. It is only to say that one can never legitimately think oneself justified in putting one's moral convictions second to any other considerations. If I think it is morally wrong to kill people, I may feel justified in fighting in a war where I have even stronger moral objections to allowing the side I disapprove of to win. But this is a typical example of a legitimate conflict internal to morality: one often has to choose between conflicting moral claims. What I cannot do is feel justified in over-riding my moral objection to killing by the consideration that war might be exciting. Or rather, if I do feel justified in this, one can infer either that I am confused or else that I attach moral worth to the pursuit of excitement.

---

[1] A different view was expressed by General Cockerill, at the War Office on 5 September 1916, when he said to Bertrand Russell: 'You and I probably regard conscience differently. I regard it as a still small voice, but when it becomes blatant and strident I suspect it of no longer being a conscience.' Quoted in Russell's *Autobiography*.

The view that moral principles must necessarily be of over-riding authority has been criticized by Mr G. J. Warnock.[1] He says that there have surely been people, and whole societies, for whom moral principles were not of great importance:

> that, perhaps, both their ideals of conduct and their actual conduct were shaped in accordance with standards that were not *moral* standards at all. Homer, in approving the ferocity, guile, and panache of the warrior chieftain, might be said to have been employing moral standards different from our own; but he might just as well, or better, be said not to have been employing moral standards at all.

Warnock's own alternative to this view is that morality should be characterized primarily in terms of its content. He says that

> it appears at least enormously plausible to say that one who professes to be making a moral judgment *must* at least profess that what is in issue is the good or harm, well-being or other-wise, of human beings – that what he regards as morally wrong is somehow damaging, and what he regards as morally right is somehow beneficial.

But it is not clear why it is better to say of Homer that he was not employing moral standards at all. There is something paro-chial in demanding that anything worthy of the name of morality should have a content similar to that of one's own. It does not appear to me 'enormously plausible' that moral judgments must concern the good or harm of human beings. While this indicates a perhaps attractive feature of a morality, it seems very unplausible to say that no judgments without this feature can be moral ones. Some moral principles are based on what is thought to be the will of some deity, without any reference to human good or harm. Warnock is aware of this argument, and rejects it:

> For I suspect that religious views differ from 'humanist' views,

1 *Contemporary Moral Philosophy*, 1967, Ch. 5. Cf. also his lecture, 'The Primacy of Practical Reason', *Proceedings of the British Academy*, 1966. For other discussions of the nature of moral beliefs, cf. the symposium on 'When is a Principle a Moral Principle?', *Proceedings of the Aristotelian Society*, Supplementary Volume, 1954; and also Frankena, *Recent Conceptions of Morality*, in Castaneda and Nakhnikian, *Morality and the Language of Conduct*, 1963.

not by denying the essential moral relevance of human benefit or harm, but rather by incorporating very different beliefs as to what really is good or bad for human beings. The religious believer finds in a supernatural order a whole extra dimension of pre-eminently important gains and losses, benefits and harm; his difference with the non-believer is not on the question whether these are of moral significance, but simply on the question whether they are real or chimerical. He might also wish to expand what might be called the moral population to include moral beings supposed not to be human; but to this, if there are such beings, no one surely will object.[1]

But this reply is hardly adequate to meet the objection. It is not clear that all religious believers attach prime moral importance to what is good or bad for humans, even when one includes their spiritual welfare and their state in any possible after-life. It is at least possible that some attach prime importance to obeying divine commands, regardless of the effect on human beings. If this point is to be met by including any deity in the 'moral population', one only needs to cite other moral beliefs that are not concerned with the well-being of humans or of gods. Many people think that cruelty to animals is morally wrong, and this view is not normally justified by appealing to the interests of people, nor by claiming that animals are 'moral beings'. Warnock's view appears to have the surely unacceptable consequence that to oppose, for its own sake, cruelty to animals cannot be a part of one's morality.

Any attempt to characterize morality primarily in terms of its content is open to the objection that the choice of what content should be required for a belief to be a moral one is bound to be arbitrary. A natural inclination may be to look at the content of one's own morality, select some very general feature of it, and to make this the central characteristic of morality itself. But how much deviation is to be permitted to other systems of belief before they lose their status as moral systems? If one's own morality is, say, that of the classical utilitarians, how many alternative moralities can one recognize? Can beliefs based wholly on divine commands, regardless of human welfare, be moral? Or beliefs about the desirability of promoting the interests of one race at the

1 *Op. cit.,* note 27.

expense of others? Or beliefs about the inviolability of sacred animals? How about a belief in the duty to perform a sacred ritual, not coupled with any beliefs about its consequences? There seems no good reason for drawing the frontier of morality in one place rather than another.

The view that, among beliefs about what one ought to do, only those count as moral that are of over-riding authority, is open to the charge that it lets some very odd beliefs into the realm of morality. But, as any social anthropologist could testify, there are some very odd moral beliefs.

A person who seriously accepts as part of his morality a duty to obey orders or to increase scientific knowledge whatever the consequences, may have adopted a position from which he cannot be dislodged by argument. For, notoriously, there are severe limits to the power of argument in moral disagreement. For some purposes, it is helpful to regard systems of moral beliefs as being like geometrical systems. In his autobiography, Russell recounts his childhood enthusiasm for geometry. He describes the distress that threatened to ruin his pleasure, when he found that the whole basis seemed to be without justification, in that the axioms themselves were not susceptible of proof. Some people feel a similar distress, made much of in the rhetoric of existentialism, when they find that moral arguments also need premises which they do not themselves prove.

Normally one's moral beliefs are far less coherent and systematic than any deductive system in mathematics or logic. But the use of a deductive system as an ideal model for a set of moral beliefs is not altogether misleading. For, like a geometrical one, a moral system can be 'refuted' only by being shown to be inconsistent. If I justify my opposition to abortion by appealing to the basic principle that one ought under no circumstances to destroy human life, you may point out that I am not an absolute pacifist. In the interests of consistency, I must then modify my basic principle or else change my mind about pacifism. But if all my moral beliefs are consistent, however objectionable they may be, there is no way in which logic can compel me to change them.

Yet, not all rational moral persuasion consists in exposure of inconsistencies.[1] Sometimes it consists in pointing to previously

1 Non-rational moral persuasion is typified by some of the kinds of manipulation discussed in a previous chapter.

unnoticed consequences of a person's principles, and asking if he really finds these consequences acceptable. Or it can consist in an appeal to experience or to the imagination, to persuade someone to change his mind about what is acceptable. There is nothing like a visit to a prison to change one's ideas about acceptable punishments. Or, to take an equally crude example, one might challenge someone's view that nuclear war could be morally acceptable by showing him a film of the victims of Hiroshima. It is only an extreme aestheticism, or an extreme philistinism, that denies that this moral role can be one of the functions of films, novels, plays or sometimes paintings. (The view that this is their sole function is a different kind of philistinism.)

3 A NARROW VIEW OF MORALITY

The word 'moral' like 'theoretical', is often contrasted with 'practical'. Remarks like 'I know there are moral objections to it, but here we must be guided by practical considerations' are parallel to others like 'It is all right in theory, but it would not work in practice.'

The alleged contrast between the theoretical and the practical is often cited, but sometimes it is hard to see what this contrast comes to. It may be that the best available explanatory or predictive theory is too limited in scope, or too unsophisticated, to be applied successfully to a particular situation. A model in economics may be of this kind, so that, although it is a good model by current standards, one may suspect that it does not take account of all the factors that influence the outcome of a real situation. But it is sometimes unclear whether the claim 'it is all right in theory but it would not work in practice' is making a possibly legitimate claim about the inadequacy of a particular theory, or is expressing a confused belief about the general relation of theory to practice. This confused belief would be in a more radical contrast between theory and practice, such that a theory might reach a theoretically adequate degree of sophistication or completeness and yet still in practice be an unreliable guide to events within its scope. But this view can be briefly dismissed: it is logically impossible for an explanatory theory to be completely adequate and yet for its predictions not to be fulfilled 'in practice'.[1] Crudely, the criterion of an empirical belief being 'all right in theory' is that it should work in practice.

But the supposed contrast between what is moral and what is practical requires more discussion. If the account given here of moral beliefs is accepted, it will be apparent that the view that moral considerations can legitimately be subordinated to other ones called 'practical' is confused. Moral beliefs about what ought to be done just are those which one accepts cannot legitimately be subordinated to any except other moral beliefs.

The view that there is in principle a gulf between theory and practice may result from supposing that the inadequacies of certain theories are a necessary feature of any theory. Similarly, the contrast between the moral and the practical may result from thinking of 'morality' in terms of some particular set of crude moral beliefs. It is common to think of morality as a series of arbitrary commands or rules, like etiquette. It may be thought to consist in apparently random injunctions, prohibiting such varied types of conduct as lying, pre-martial sex, or getting into debt, often without any obvious general justification in terms of human benefit or harm. It is natural that, when the content of the morality they are taught is rigid and crude, people may see adherence to its rules as a relatively low priority. Such rules in their arbitrariness resemble a code of etiquette, and do not come with any compelling reasons for being taken more seriously.

In this way, the crude view of morality as a set of commands, immune from criticism and devoid of justification, leaves room for the belief that one can legitimately allow non-moral considerations to over-ride moral ones. This belief is that tacitly invoked by patriots, soldiers, scientists or others who claim to inhabit a realm of activity outside the scope of morality. Words like 'orders' or 'science' are used to ward off moral criticism like a magic spell. This separation between morality and practice can function as a defence mechanism in two separate ways. It can enable an agent to think that he escapes the moral responsibility for his action, and

1 The supposed contrast was criticized in 1793, by Kant in his paper 'On the saying: That may be all right in Theory but it is no good in Practice'. The even more naïve view that being 'practical' consists in doing without any theory invites the *ad hominem* retort of Keynes: 'Practical men, who believe themselves to be quite exempt from any intellectual influences, are usually the slaves of some defunct economist.'

at the same time it can protect his 'morality' from the modifying influence of experience. The view of morality presupposed can only be undermined by philosophical argument.

Someone who holds a narrow or peculiar set of basic moral beliefs, but who is consistent, and also unyielding to the modifying influences of experience or imagination, is beyond the reach of argument. If I insist that an absolute duty to obey orders, or to extend scientific knowledge, is a basic postulate of my moral system, you may be unable to persuade me rationally that I should change my view.[1] But the role of moral fanatic is an unattractive one, so that I may well desire to hold moral beliefs of a more appealing kind and yet to justify restricting the scope of morality. But, if you then persuade me by philosophical argument that an adequate conception of morality rules out such restriction, I am then unable, except by gross evasion, to escape from a choice between principles.

A man who has tried to keep his 'morality' in an isolated compartment of his life may perhaps be a soldier, who claims that it includes the command 'thou shalt not kill'. He may have said that, as a soldier, he sees that he ought not to let his morality interfere with such practical considerations as the need to obey orders. But, if he can be persuaded that this belief is incoherent (since, by definition, his morality is the set of his beliefs to which he thinks over-riding priority ought to be given) he is faced with a choice. He may blatantly evade the choice by refusing to consider the matter further; but, without such evasion, he must either make an admission or else revise his beliefs. He may admit that, if he obeys orders going against his stated moral principles, his action is wrong and cannot be justified. Or, he may revise the claims made about his own morality, recognizing that in it obedience to orders occupies a more significant place than the commands to which he has paid lip service.

A man confronted with such a choice may prefer, rather than to accept criticism of his conduct, to adopt the perhaps unappealing beliefs required to justify it. But, to remain convinced of these beliefs, it may be necessary to do more than ensure that they are

---

1 This is the morality that Hegel likened to 'the spiritual zoo', in which we are each confined in our separate cages. (As yet I have read very little Hegel: I came across this in Professor MacIntyre's stimulating *Short History of Ethics*.)

consistent. It may well be necessary to isolate them from any emotional appreciation of their consequences. War-like politicians do not visit hospitals for wounded children; judges are not often seen at prisons. At least since Orwell, it is a truism that we use language in such a way as to deaden our emotional awareness of the consequences of our actions and beliefs. At a commonplace level, we help ourselves to forget that we kill animals for food by renaming cow as 'beef' and sheep as 'mutton'. At another level, we hide from the realities of war by inventing a jargon to disguise killing ('mopping up operations', etc.) and to de-humanize those who are killed ('Viet Cong', 'imperialists', etc.). To varying degrees, most of us evade emotional awareness of the consequences of our beliefs or actions. But a further line of defence is to claim that this exclusion of emotional response is necessary or even desirable. 'Realism' in discussing the rights and wrongs of a war is said to consist in discussing such factors as the balance of power, economic considerations or strategy, and in the rigid exclusion of such 'emotionalism' as mentioning the agonies caused by Napalm bombs.

But, on the account of moral reasoning proposed here, this further line of defence can be seen to be illegitimate. 'Emotional' descriptions of suffering are relevant to moral argument, for, if one cannot accept as justified the consequences of one's principles, one cannot logically retain those principles unmodified.

4 A POSSIBLE OBJECTION

It may be objected that I have ruled out the 'narrow view' of morality dogmatically, merely by defining 'morality' to suit my own convenience. As the argument stands, this objection has some force. The very fact that some people do hold the narrow view that has been criticized is some evidence that the account of 'morality' proposed here is not based on any universally accepted way of using the word. It has been argued by some philosophers that the concept of morality is one about which there must inevitably be disagreements.[1] But, even if one is uncertain

1 E.g. by Professor Hampshire, *Thought and Action*, 1959, pp. 230–231. Later (p. 240) he says, 'One of the few universally accepted connotations of the word "moral" is "important": no moral question can also be trivial, and not worth careful consideration.'

how such a claim could be established, it is plausible to claim that there is not at present general agreement as to the scope of the concept.

In such cases of disputed concepts, evidence of how words are used only determines some of the limits that should be observed in giving an account of a concept. It is unhelpful to characterize morality in a way so perverse that one's use of the word deviates radically from most normal uses. It is thus legitimate to argue against a characterization of a concept that such an account gives rise to paradoxes. Thus, to define 'morality' in terms of rules concerning sex would have the paradoxical consequence that few of the normal objections to war would count as moral ones. But, where concepts are disputed, it may be that either several rival accounts all avoid violent clashes with ordinary usage, or that none do. Then, one may wish to abandon the word altogether, or to admit a plurality of uses as equally legitimate, or to provide arguments other than lexical ones in favour of a stipulative account.

The view proposed here, that where I hold a belief about what I ought to do this only counts as one of my moral beliefs if I admit that it ought to have a certain priority, is based on a stipulative account of 'morality'. It was suggested that certain other views led to paradoxical conclusions, but no argument was offered that any possible alternative view must clash with ordinary uses of the word. The case for this stipulative account ultimately rests on the view that, for purposes of moral argument, this is the most useful way of using the word. No doubt this view in turn rests on moral assumptions with which people could disagree.

Some people may wish to reject the account of the word 'morality' proposed here. If so, the essential thesis of this chapter need not be undermined, although it will need reformulating. I am not here concerned with the word 'morality' for its own sake, but rather concerned with those beliefs about what one ought to do which have the kind of priority described. Where these beliefs are not those which one describes as one's moral beliefs, certain questions arise. How can one justify relegating one's 'morality' to subordinate place? If one can justify this, perhaps because one's 'morality' consists of rules that are trivial or arbitrary, this 'morality' seems to have the same status as a set of rules of etiquette. And, if this is so, why should one not abandon it?

5 'COMMON SENSE' AND PHILOSOPHICAL CRITICISM

Discussions of the evasion of moral issues normally concentrate on a kind of wilful distortion or overlooking of facts. Typical is Sartre's description of a woman being seduced, who at each stage evades the significance of what is happening, or tells herself that she will stop soon but not yet, until finally it is too late.[1] Freud's view of the unconscious involved him in what are in effect descriptions of self-deception, and again this consists in evasion or distortion of fact, whether about the world or about one's own motives. But there is also a variety of moral evasion that depends on the distorting effects of the categories and assumptions in terms of which one thinks. This distortion can function by obscuring facts, but may equally well function by preventing certain questions from being raised. The narrow view of morality already discussed is an example of this.

Such moral evasion is often defended by an appeal to 'common sense'. It is said to be a matter of common sense that a soldier must obey orders; that a citizen must obey the law; that a scientist must do his research without thinking of the consequences; that moral considerations must take second place to practical ones. To invoke common sense is to appeal to something other than evidence or argument, with the clear insinuation that intuitively obvious beliefs require no such rational support. We normally give such status only to those of our beliefs that form our most fundamental assumptions, or that seem unavoidable within the categories in terms of which we think.

But common sense about morality retreats before philosophical argument in the way that superstitions about illness retreat before medical research. For the function of philosophical criticism is to call in question the assumptions and categories that are fundamental to our social or personal systems of belief. Borrowing terms from current linguistic theory, one can make a crude (and only relative) distinction between the surface structure and the deep structure of a person's beliefs. Similarities of surface structure can obscure differences at a deeper level. Two people may go to the same church, support the same political

1 *Being and Nothingness*, Part I, Chapter 2, Section 2.

party, have the same views on a range of issues, and yet at a deeper level have fundamentally different structures of belief. For one, the fundamental political categories may be left and right, progressive and reactionary, while for the other they may be liberal and authoritarian, empirical and ideological. They may have the same surface views on capital punishment, although one thinks in terms of deterrence and the other in terms of retribution.

Philosophical criticism aims at exposing the deep structure of a system of beliefs, and then examining its fundamental assumptions and categories as though under a microscope. Often our most fundamental beliefs about how society should be arranged or how we ought to live are stated with the help of such words as 'free', 'rational', 'just', 'scientific', 'moral', 'deserved' or 'happy'. One philosophical task is to bring these words sharply into focus, so that our fundamental beliefs are less blurred and confused. Another is to make ourselves state clearly our most general beliefs, for only then can we see the extent to which they can be questioned.

If we accept the view, mentioned in connection with Eichmann, that there is a duty to submit one's conduct to moral criticism, it is hard to see how certain consequences for moral education can be avoided. One is that at the least, we must not give children an education that makes a prime virtue either of conformity or of unconditional obedience. The dangers of this are dramatized by Milgram's well-known experiment on obedience.[1] Forty men were each told that they were taking part in a study of the effects of punishment on learning. When the 'learner' gave an incorrect answer, each subject of the experiment was ordered to press a switch that he believed gave the 'learner' an electric shock. The victim was strapped to an 'electric chair' in the next room. The volunteer was made to think that by pressing different switches, he was administering increasingly severe shocks to the learner, who acted as if this were so. When the 'shock' reached 300 volts, the victim kicked on the wall. The volunteer asked for guidance and was advised to continue after a brief pause. After the 315-volt shock, the victim kicked on the wall again, but the volunteer was ordered to continue right up to the maximum of 450 volts. To reach this apparent voltage, it was necessary to pull

1 'Behavioural Study of Obedience', *Journal of Abnormal and Social Psychology*, 1963.

the switch through positions marked 'slight shock/moderate shock/strong shock/very strong shock/intense shock/extreme intensity shock/danger: severe shock/XXX (450 volts)'.

Many taking part in the experiment showed signs of great tension. Milgram says,

> Many subjects showed signs of nervousness in the experi-
> mental situation, and especially upon administering the more
> powerful shocks. In a large number of cases the degree of
> tension reached extremes that are rarely seen in sociopsycho-
> logical laboratory studies. Subjects were observed to sweat,
> tremble, stutter, bite their lips, groan, and dig their fingernails
> into their flesh. These were characteristic rather than exceptional
> responses to the experiment. One sign of tension was the
> regular occurrence of nervous laughing fits. Fourteen of the
> forty subjects showed definite signs of nervous laughter
> and smiling. The laughter seemed entirely out of place, even
> bizarre. Full-blown, uncontrollable seizures were observed
> for three subjects. On one occasion we observed a seizure so
> violently convulsive that it was necessary to call a halt to the
> experiment.

Milgram quotes one observer as saying, 'I observed a mature and initially poised business-man enter the laboratory smiling and confident. Within twenty minutes he was reduced to a twitching, stuttering wreck, who was rapidly approaching a point of nervous collapse. He constantly pulled on his earlobe, and twisted his hands. At one point he pushed his fist into his forehead and muttered: "Oh God, let's stop it." And yet he continued to respond to every word of the experimenter, and obeyed to the end.'

Although most of them showed these signs of stress, twenty-six of the forty volunteers obeyed right to the end. Only five refused to continue after the victim's first protest. It is not clear exactly how this experiment should be interpreted. We cannot be sure what was going on in the minds of those who continued to administer what they thought were electric shocks, any more than we can be sure what goes on in a psychologist's mind as he continues an experiment that reduces someone to 'a twitching, stuttering wreck'. But it is hard not to see the behaviour of those who took part in the experiment as illustrating a widespread Eichmann-like capacity for misplaced obedience.

But the belief in a duty to submit conduct to moral criticism has another consequence for education. It is important, not only to discourage mindless conformity or obedience, but also to combat the evasion that depends on thinking being distorted by inadequate categories and concepts. And this requires that the techniques of philosophical criticism are made a central part of education, as are the techniques of scientific enquiry. Children in schools are taught to expect that 'common sense' factual beliefs may be proved wrong by scientific experiment, and we try to give them the ability to test empirical beliefs themselves. But, if the arguments of this chapter are accepted, it is also desirable that they should be taught to lay bare the deep structure of their own or their society's moral and political beliefs, and should be taught how to criticize them. 'Common sense' about morality or politics just as much as about the physical world, can be destroyed by rational enquiry. There seems no good reason why education should not include the discovery of this.

10

CONCLUSIONS

The most persistent problems in philosophy often turn out not to consist in one question to which there is a single correct answer. They can sometimes instead be a tangled knot of questions of different kinds, each of which may require for its solution different methods of enquiry. The problem of free will has been one of the most persistent and stubborn of philosophical issues largely because it is a combination of conceptual questions, as yet un-answered empirical questions, and very fundamental evaluative questions. The problem often presents itself as a clash between the apparent claims of science on the one hand and of morality on the other. It is said that Kant saw the problems as important partly because he wished to reconcile his admiration for Newton with his admiration for Rousseau. We seem to be torn between our commitment to the methods of science and our commitment to deeply rooted attitudes towards other people and ourselves.

The argument of this book has been stated partly by discussing certain disputed concepts. Among these have been 'responsibility', 'conscience', 'mental illness' and 'morality'. In part, the proposed accounts of these words are openly stipulative: if some people use the expression 'mental illness' so that any 'deviance' comes within its scope, then it is time they stopped doing so. But not everyone will accept the accounts given of these concepts. However, the central argument of the book can be stated in a way that is largely independent of them. I have tried to break down the free will problem into a number of separate questions and to suggest how they might be answered.

In Chapter 2 it was argued that the question of whether or not all human behaviour is governed by causal laws is an empirical one, which should be left to scientists to solve, if they can. Part of the stubborn nature of the whole problem derives from the fact that this is a very difficult empirical question which we are still far from answering.

Then there are moral questions about the justification of blame and of some kinds of praise. Since unreasonable praise seems at worst a minor evil, the discussion has concentrated upon when, if ever, blame is legitimate. It was argued in the third and fourth chapters that blame may serve a useful purpose in influencing what people do, and that various different excuses may be offered by saying 'I could not help it'. Aristotle, with reservations, said blame was unreasonable when the agent acted in ignorance or under constraint. I have taken a similar view, but have emphasized inner 'constraints' that diminish one's capacities just as surely as external ones diminish one's opportunities. These inner constraints can be seen operating in any case of compulsive or addictive behaviour. They can be divided into those that reduce or remove my ability to form or alter an intention, and those that reduce or remove my ability to put my intention into effect.

It was suggested that there are essentially two kinds of justification for our accepting most of the excuses that we do: in these cases blame is often (though not always) pointless, and in these cases it is always unjust. The conceptual question as to the nature of justice and injustice was briefly discussed in terms of the links between what someone deserves and his abilities and opportunities. It was argued that blame only functions in the context of our identifying a person with his 'intentions' rather than with his abilities and opportunities. Where a wrong act was not the result of a bad intention, but was rather the result of lack of ability or opportunity to do anything else, we think it unfair to blame the agent. It was argued, against 'hard' determinists, that the truth of determinism would not make blame usually pointless. Nor would it make blame always unfair, for it was claimed that determinism is compatible with our having the capacity and the opportunity to do otherwise than we do.

Related to questions about the justification of blame and excuses are other moral questions about the justification of punishment and excuses.[1] I argued in Chapter 8 that punishment is an evil, and very likely in many cases not a necessary one. On the moral approach proposed, a sufficiently imaginative policy of social experiment should substantially reduce, and perhaps altogether eliminate, legal punishment. If the proposed moral restrictions were taken seriously, we should be likely at least to tear down our prisons. But some penalties might well still be necessary. (Whether or not they would is an empirical question we have not yet tried to answer.) If so, they should be regarded as unfair in just those cases where blame is unfair: these include all cases where the lawbreaker lacked the capacity or opportunity to do other than he did. And the unfairness of a punishment is a powerful reason, though not always a conclusive one, for not administering it.

But it is not enough to talk in general terms of someone having the ability and opportunity to act differently. Supporters of 'soft' determinism have often pointed out that determinism does not entail that all actions are done at gunpoint. But this contrast between most actions and a few actions done under heavy, crude and obvious external pressure is not denied by 'hard' determinists. Perhaps because they have been more concerned to defend the effectiveness of blame than to defend its fairness, soft determinists have repeatedly pointed to our opportunities to act in various ways, without saying much about the limits set on our abilities. The varieties of external pressures upon us are relatively clear; but, as lawyers and psychiatrists have found, the extent to which internal pressures limit our abilities is much less easy to discern.

Since it is a central thesis of this book that determinism does not entail that we are always unable to act differently from how we do act, it has seemed necessary to look at the boundaries of our abilities more closely. The hardest problems arise over the abilities of the mentally ill, and among these problems the most stubborn of all concern psychopaths, who are said to lack a conscience. I tried, in Chapter 5, to give an account of the abilities necessary for one to be said to possess a conscience. In Chapters 6 and 7, an

1   There are important differences between legal and moral responsibility that arise from the fact that the law often demands clear-cut answers where moral judgments have blurred boundaries. Hart and Honoré point out (in *Causation in the Law*, 1961) that a man who negligently starts a fire in New York is only liable to pay for the first house it burns down. Similarly, in English law, a man is not guilty of murder unless his victim dies within a year and a day.

attempt was made to give an account of the concept of mental illness, in a way that is not open to some recent attacks on the concept, and to trace some of the relevant links between being mentally ill and having impaired abilities. It was argued that possession of abilities is often not an all-or-none affair, and that our abilities can be diminished to varying degrees. The best way of thinking of the degree of impairment in any particular case is to consider the amount of persuasion that would be necessary to alter the person's conduct.

It was claimed that, if there is a distinction between those acts that result from diminished opportunities or capacities and those that do not, it is up to us to choose whether to make blame and punishment depend on it. We could have a world in which no one was ever blamed or punished. We could, less attractively, retain blame and punishment (or perhaps 'blame' and 'punishment') but not confine them to those cases where the wrongdoer could help what he did. But, if one is dissatisfied with these alternatives, one is entitled to retain the links between blame and punishment, on the one hand, and abilities and opportunities on the other. This option is a genuine one only if it is possible to explain the difference between 'normal' actions and those that result from diminished opportunities and abilities.

In Chapter 9, I discussed some pleas of non-responsibility that seem to me unacceptable. It was suggested that undesirable attempts to evade responsibility often depend on not questioning certain inadequate or confused concepts and categories of thought. The difference between clear and confused thinking about fundamental beliefs and concepts is not just an academic matter. It affects our attitudes to actions and to people, including ourselves. And our attitudes affect our own actions.

INDEX

Index

Index